Printed in the United States Of America

ISBN: 978-1-365-62258-8

Contact@ ateaford@gmail.com

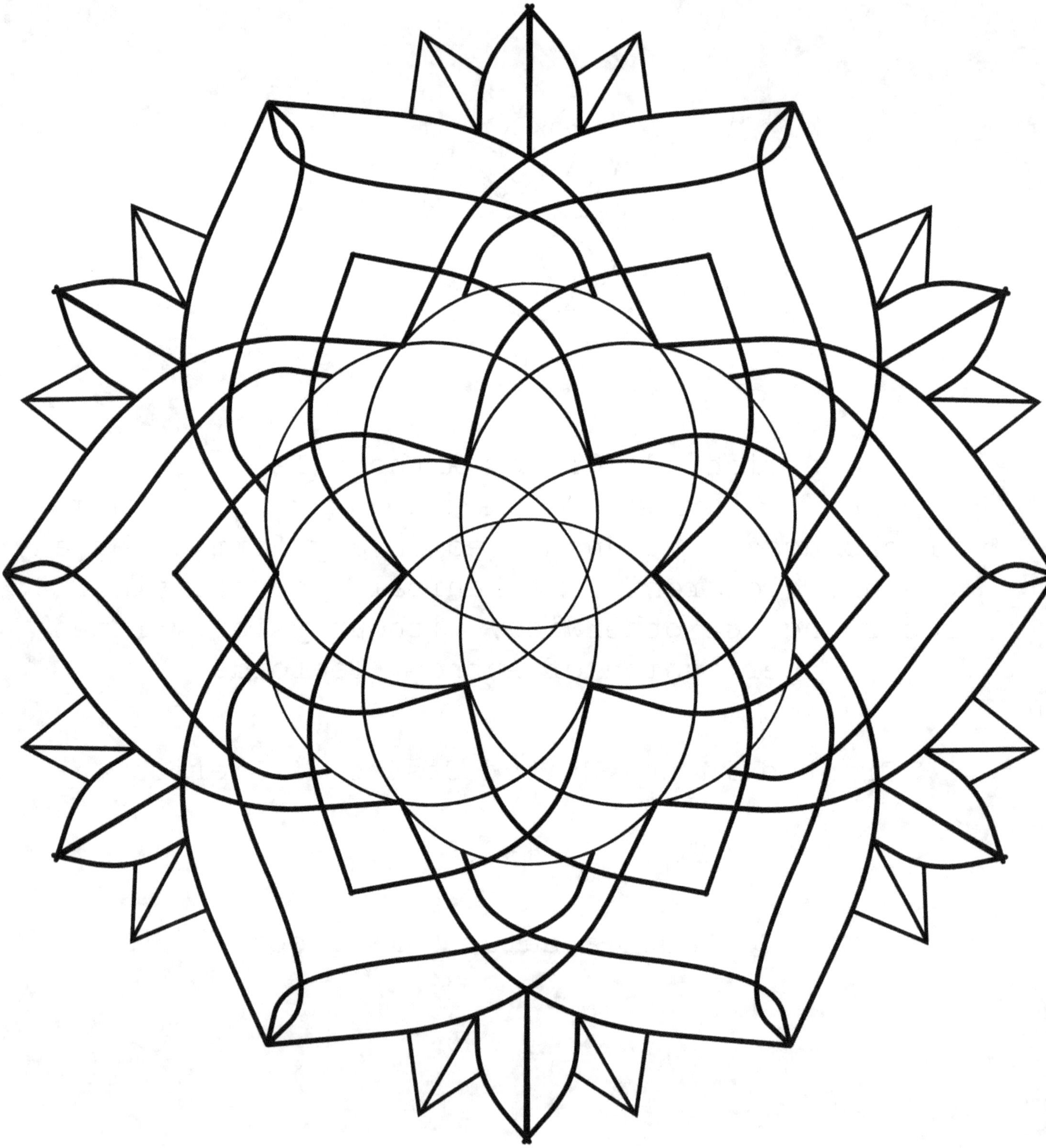

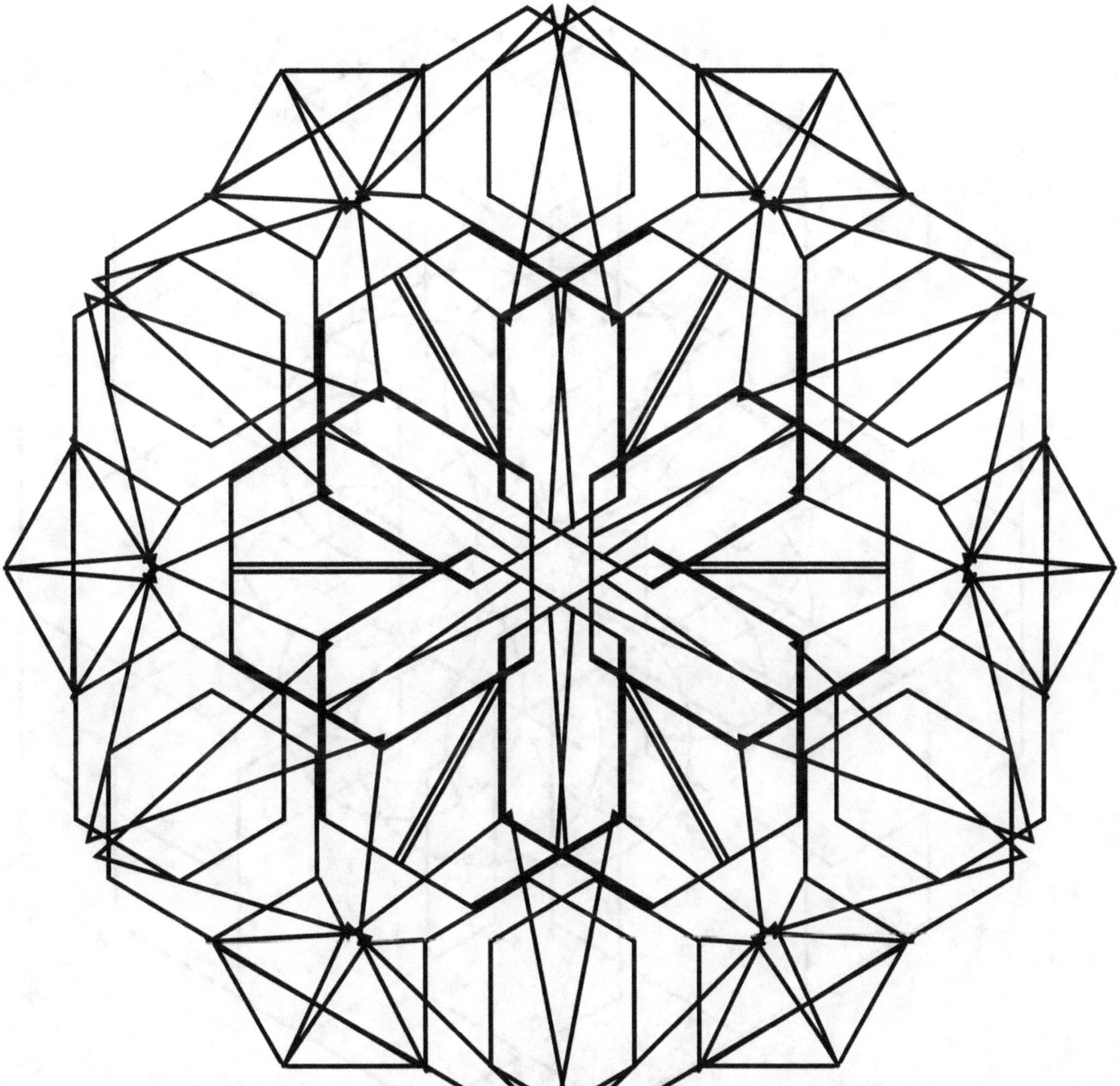

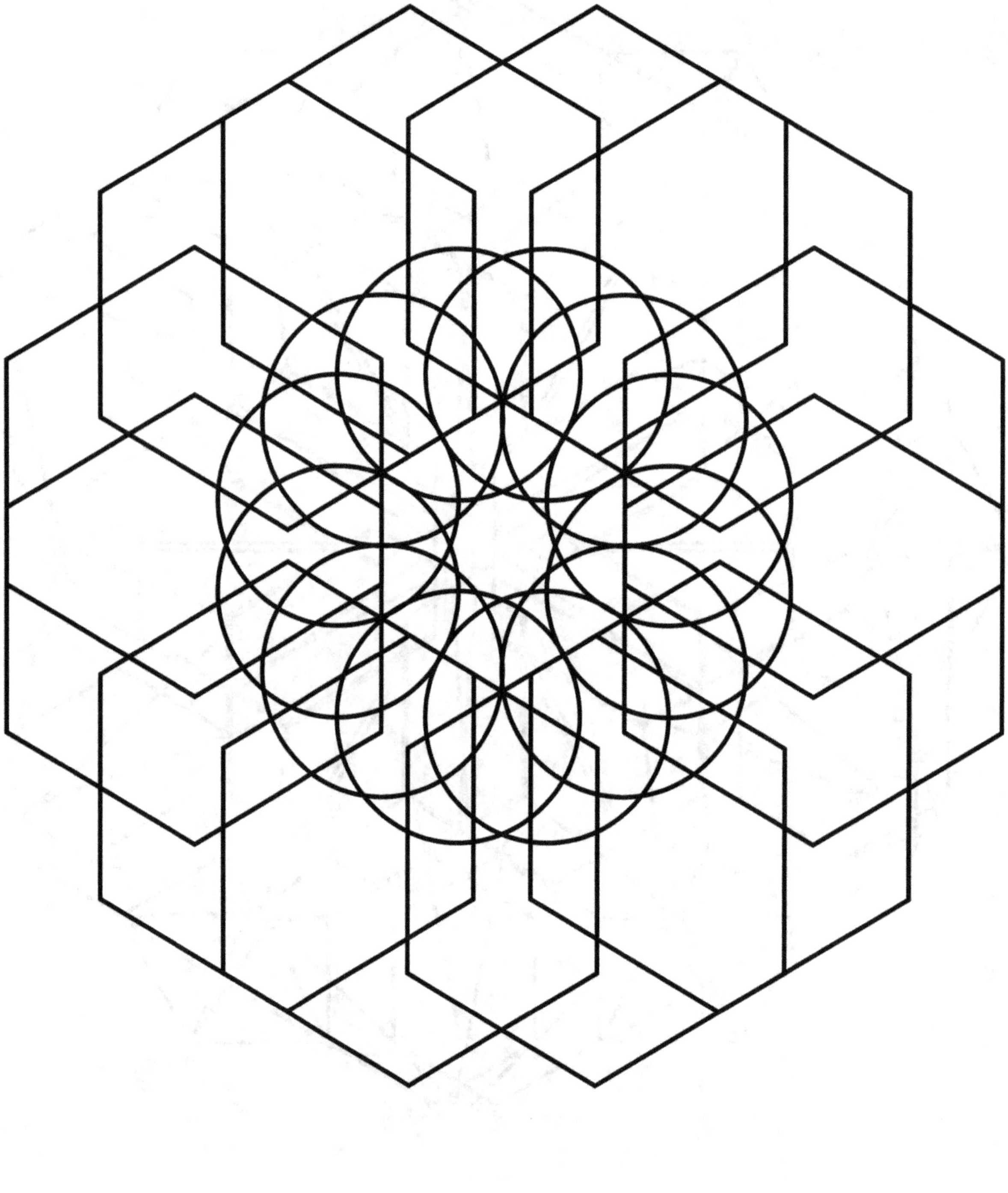

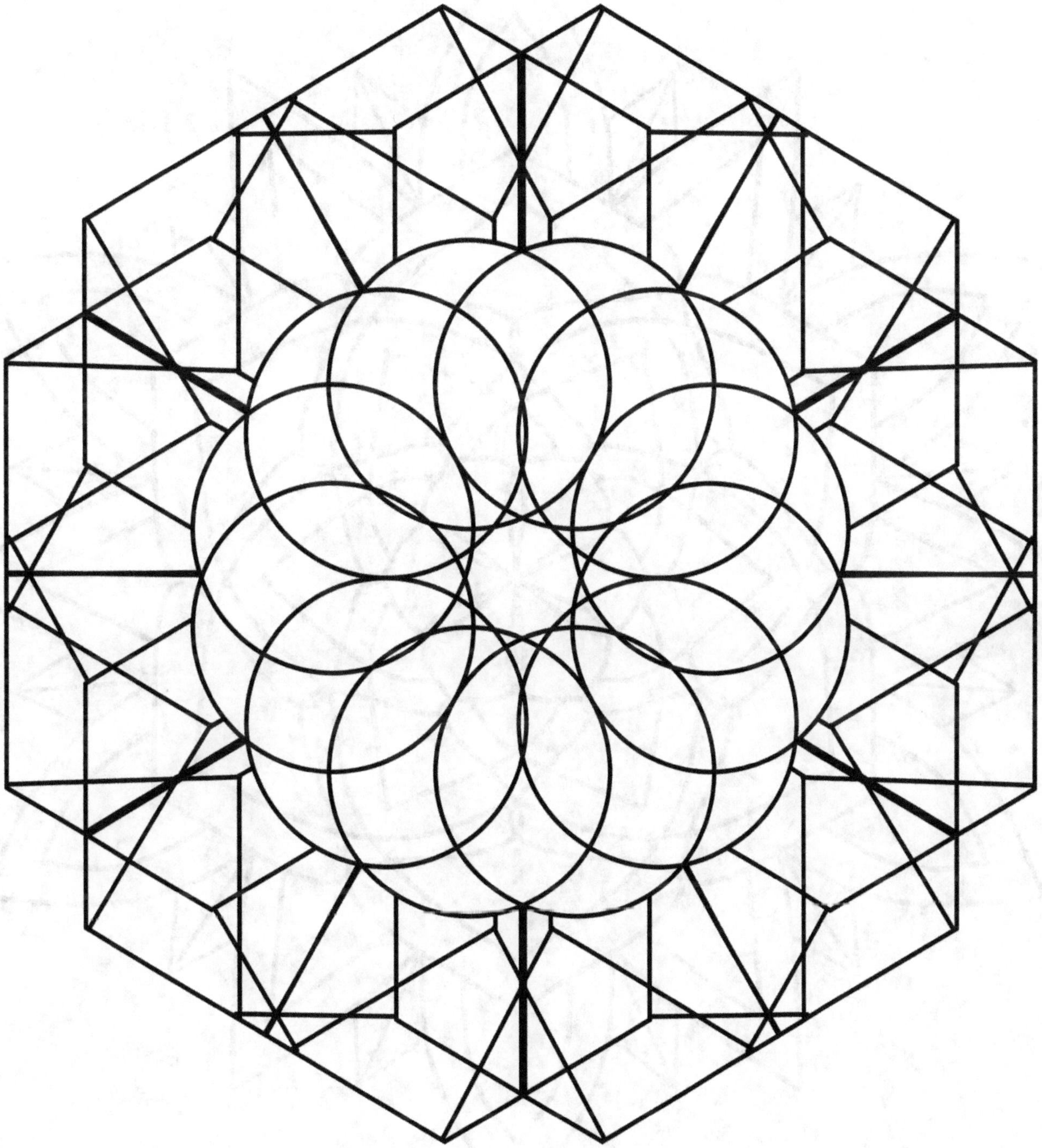

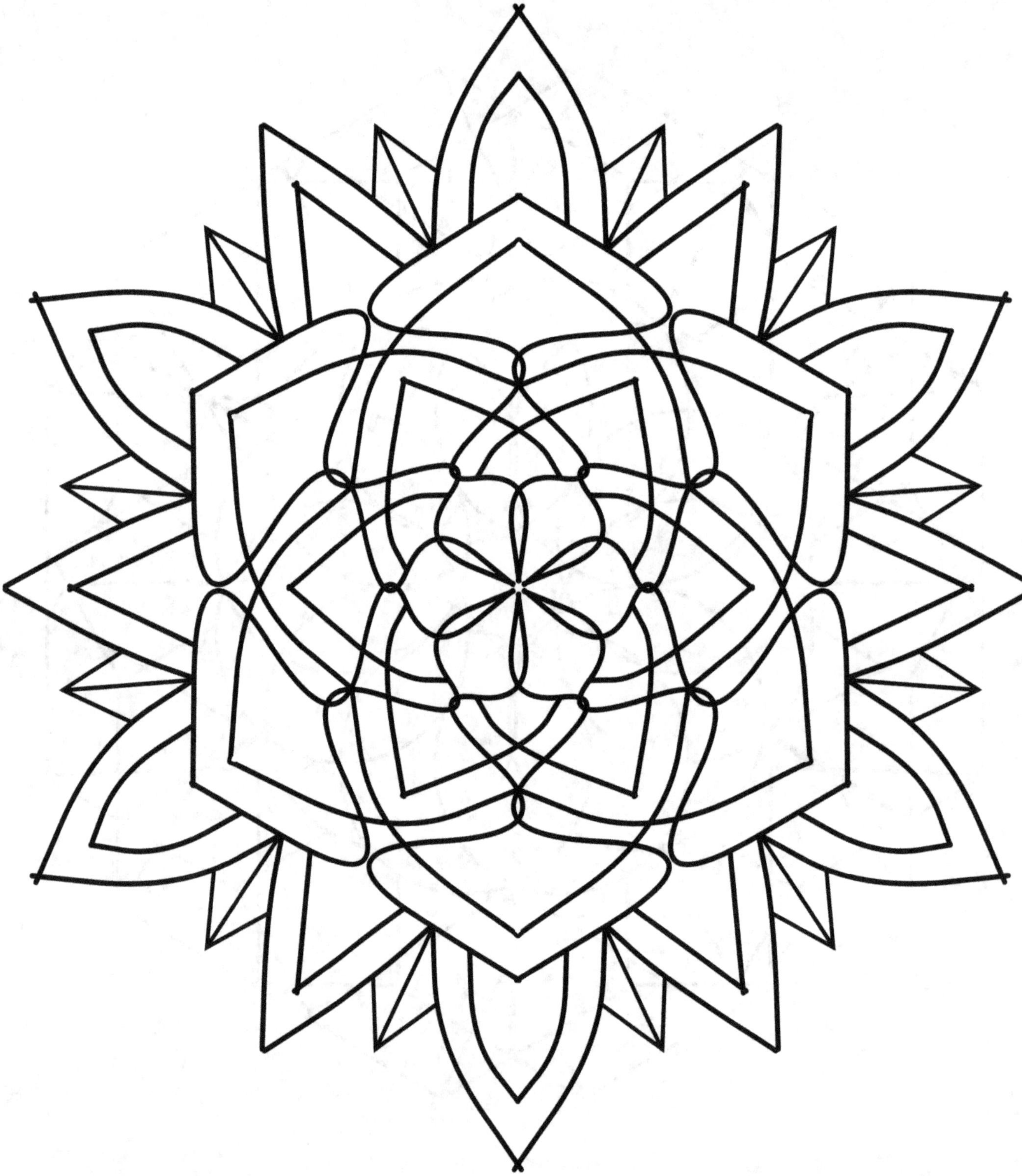

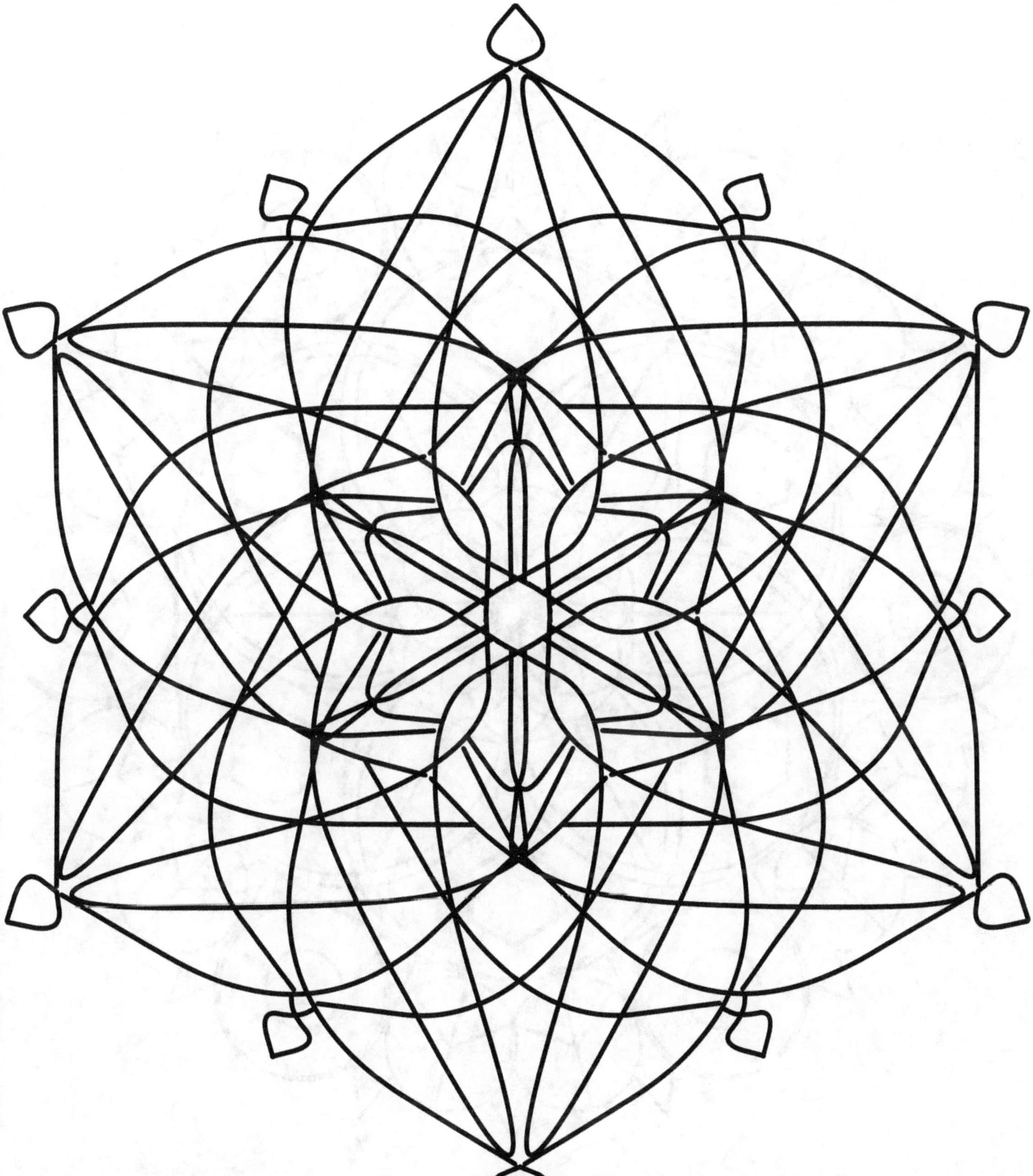

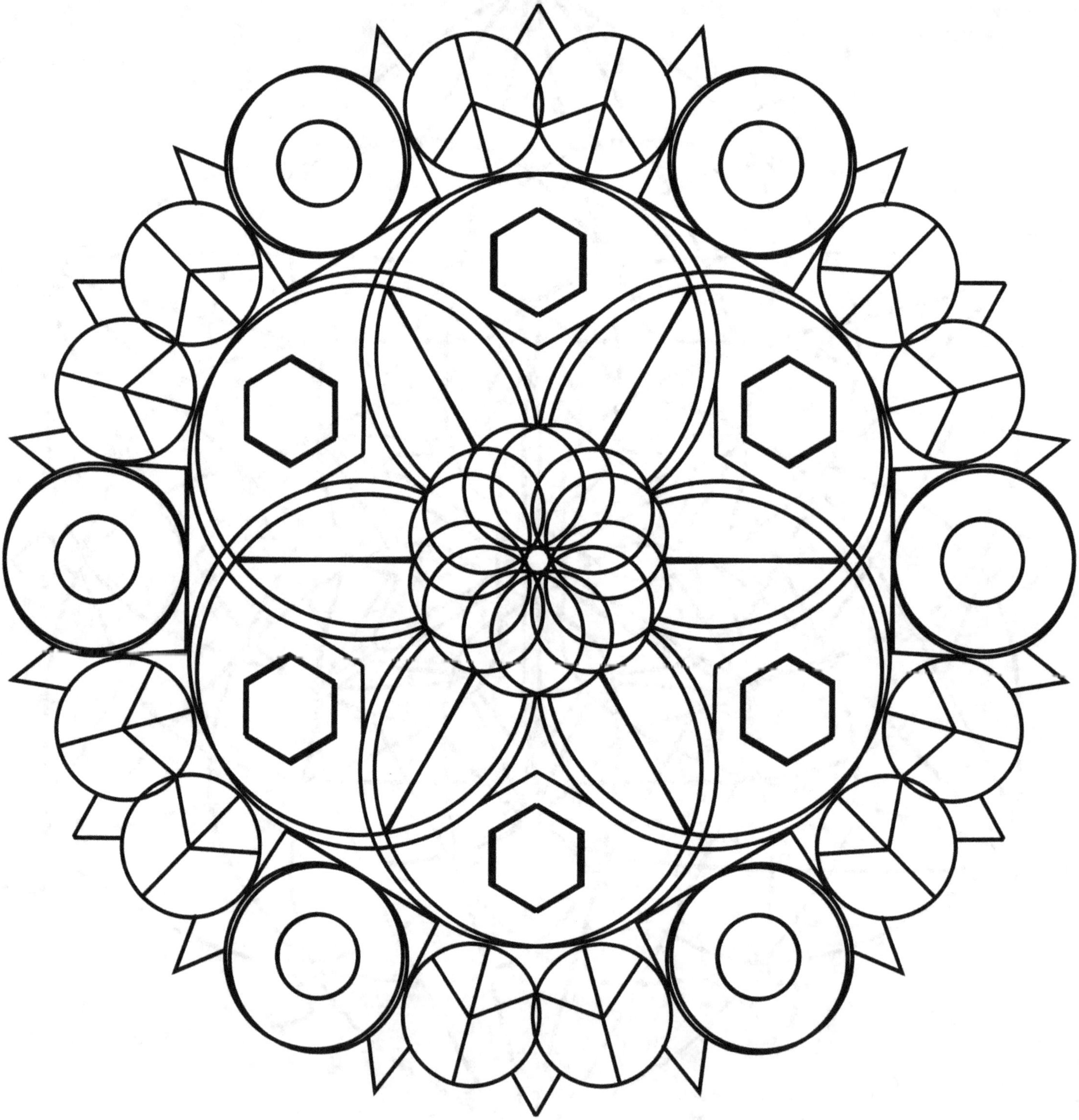

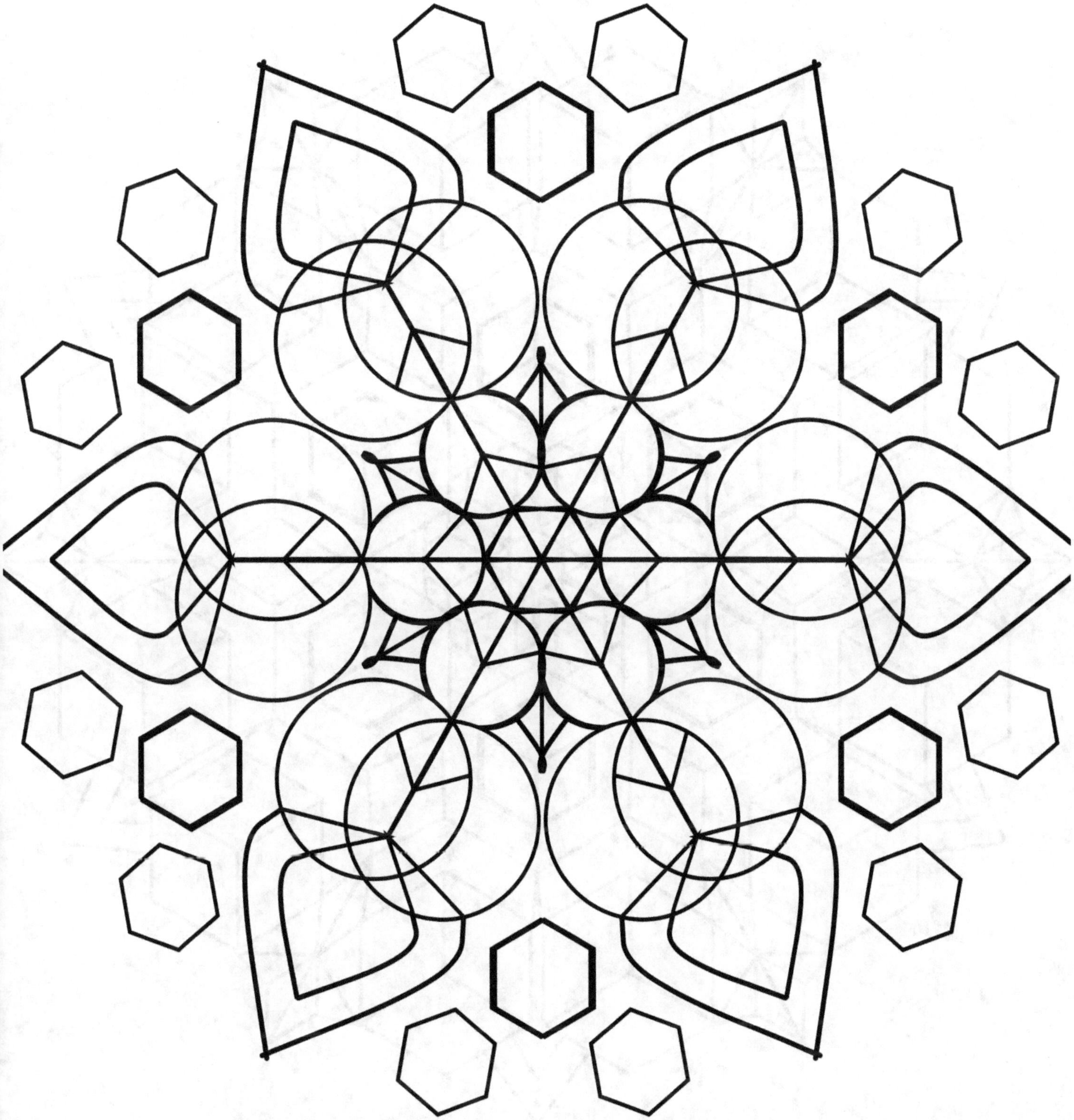

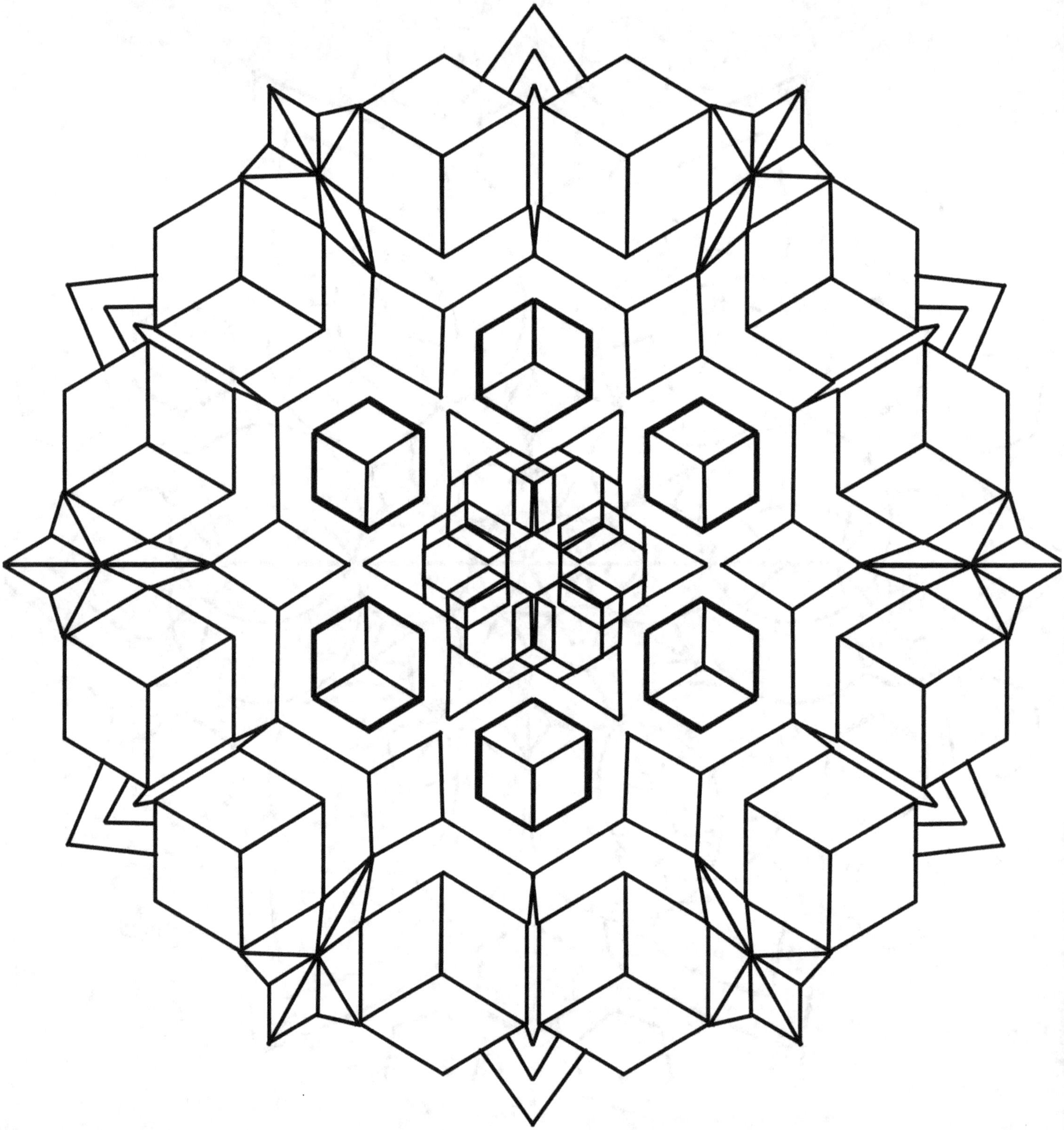

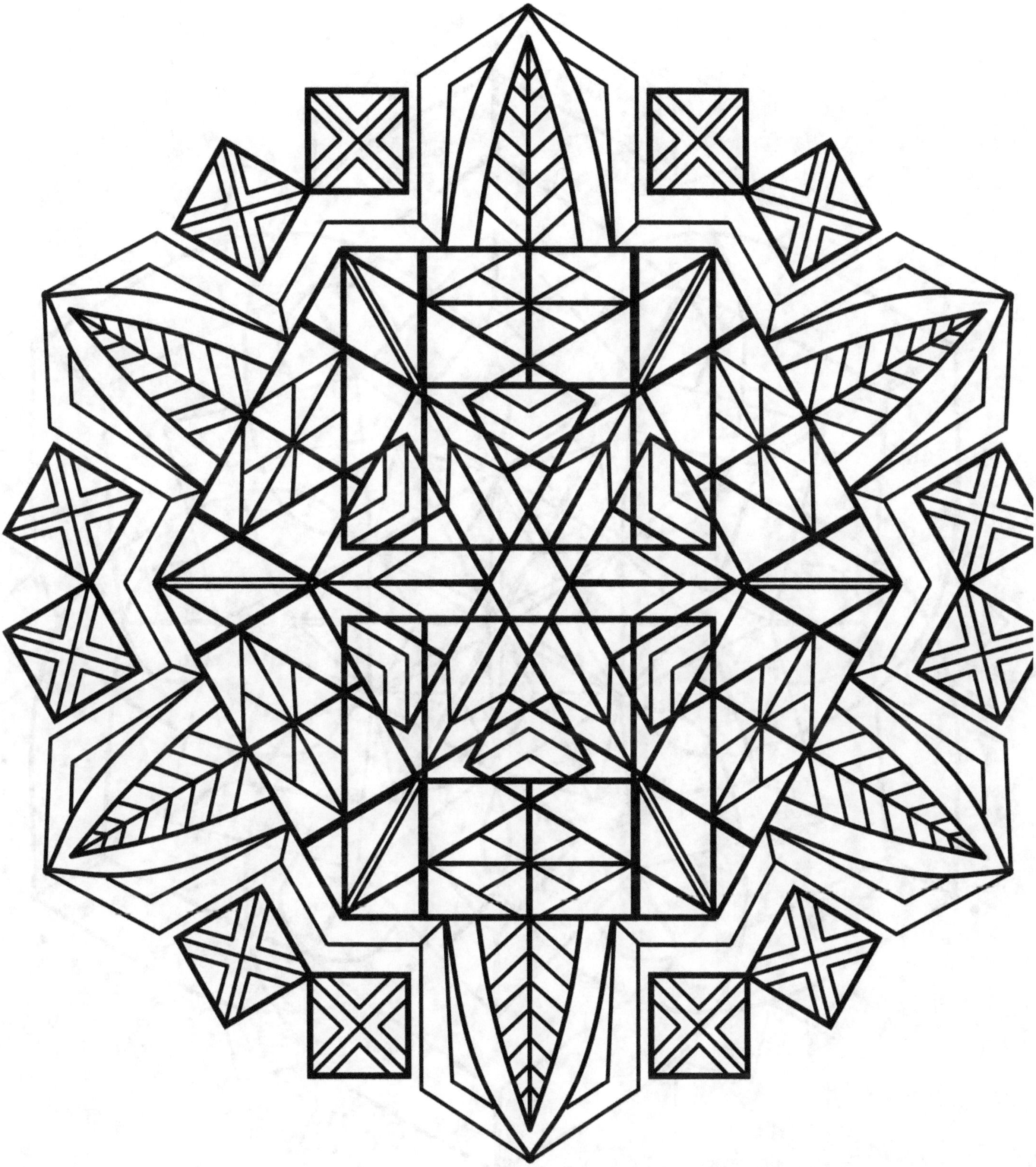

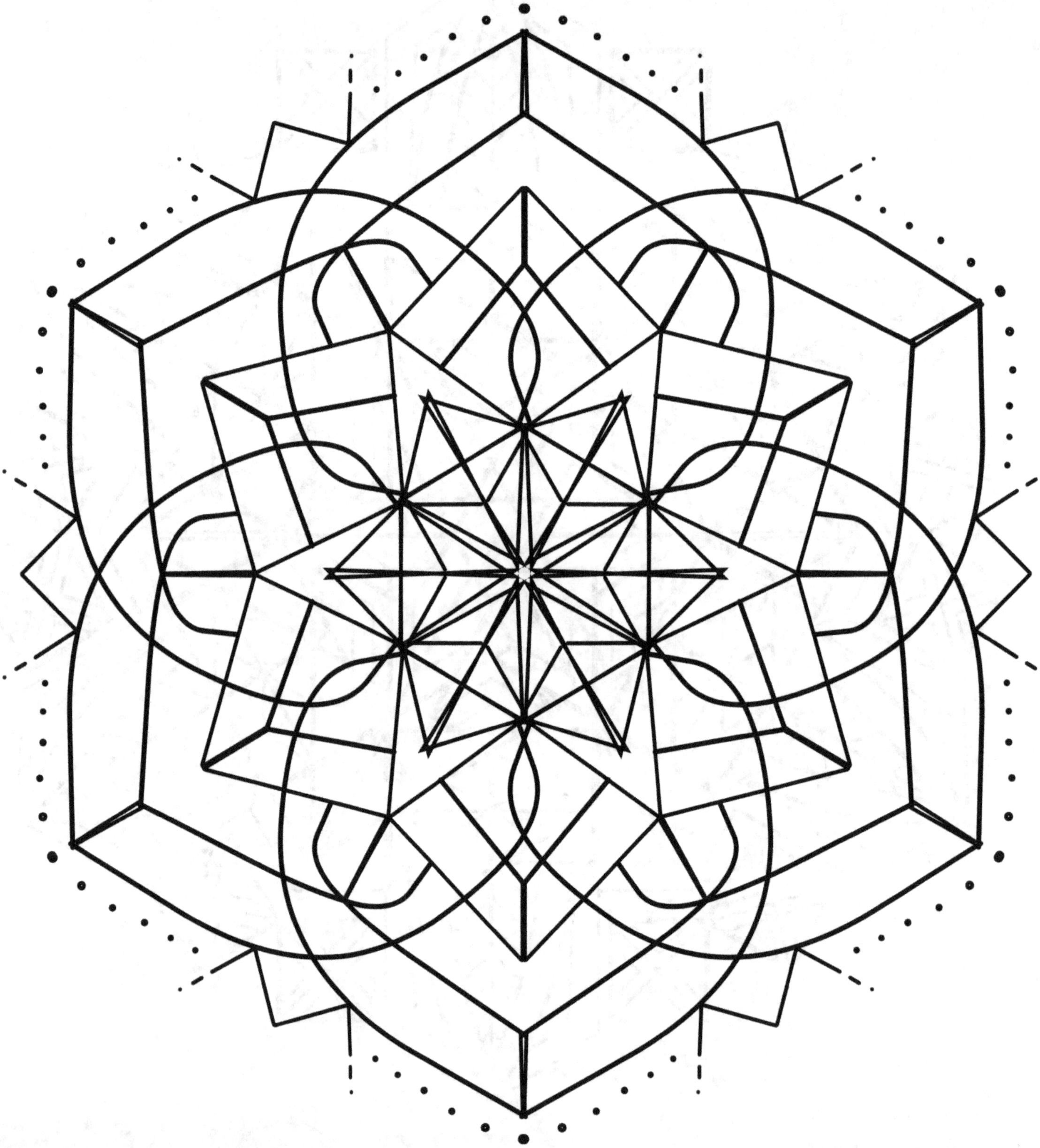

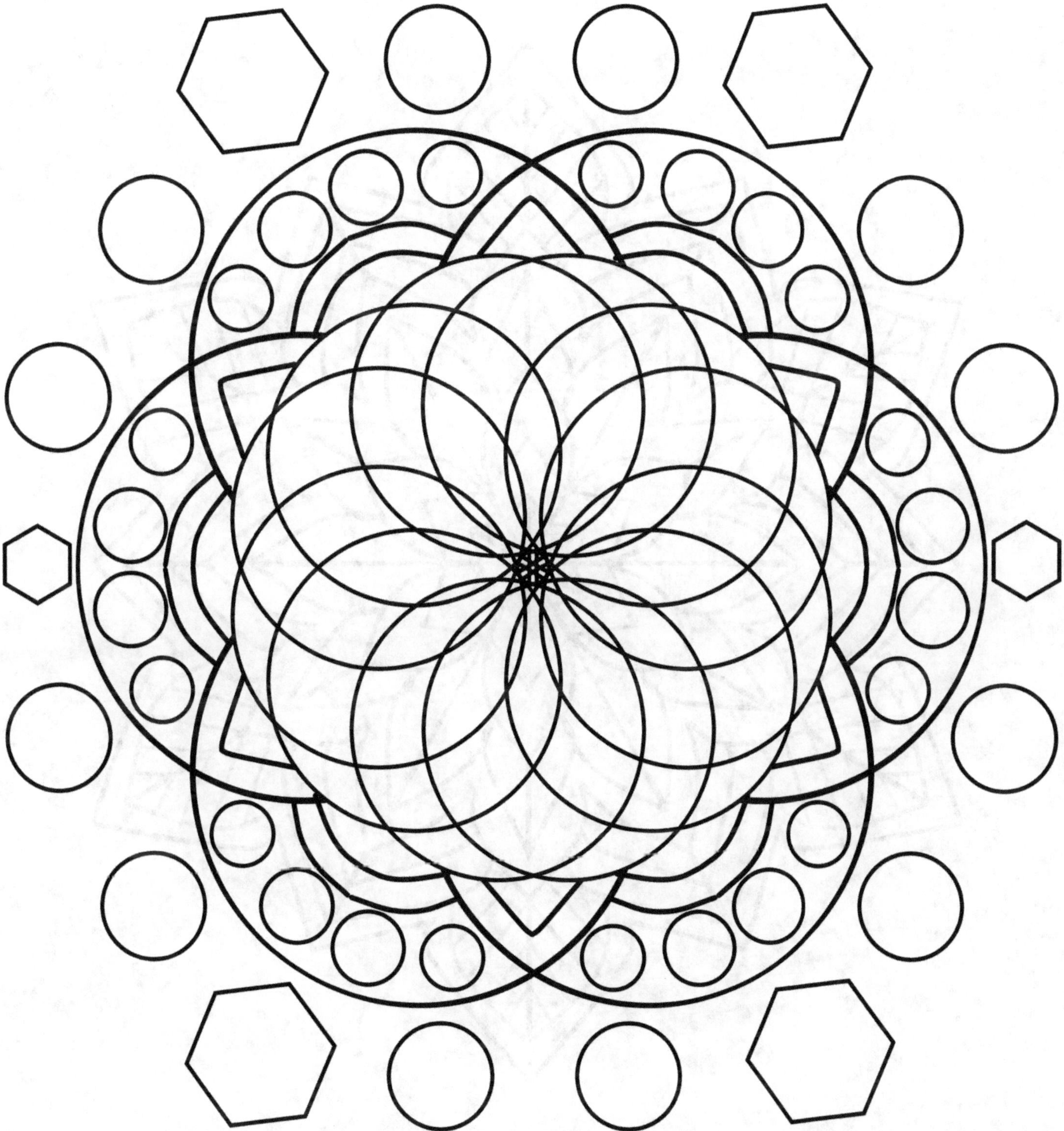

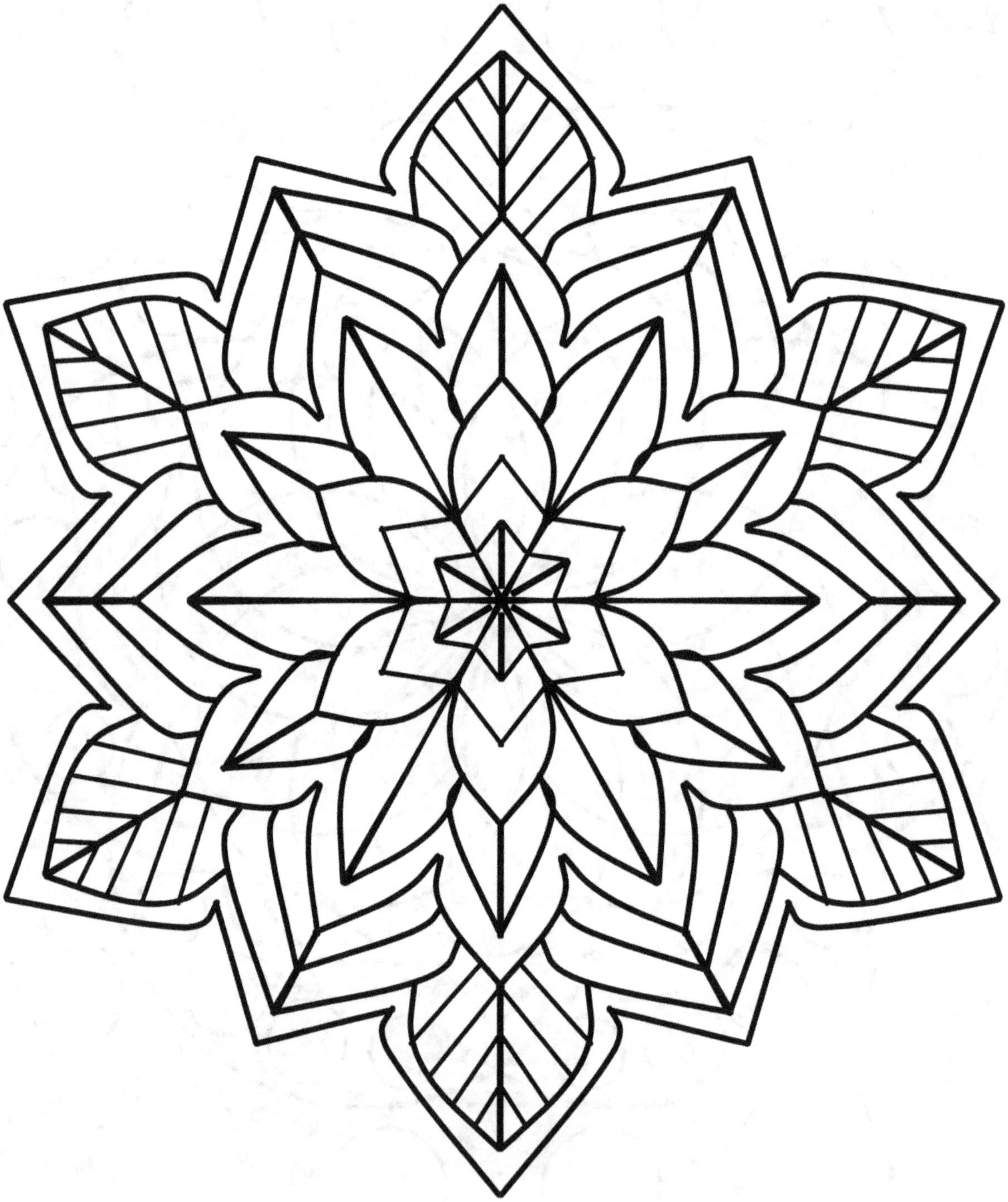

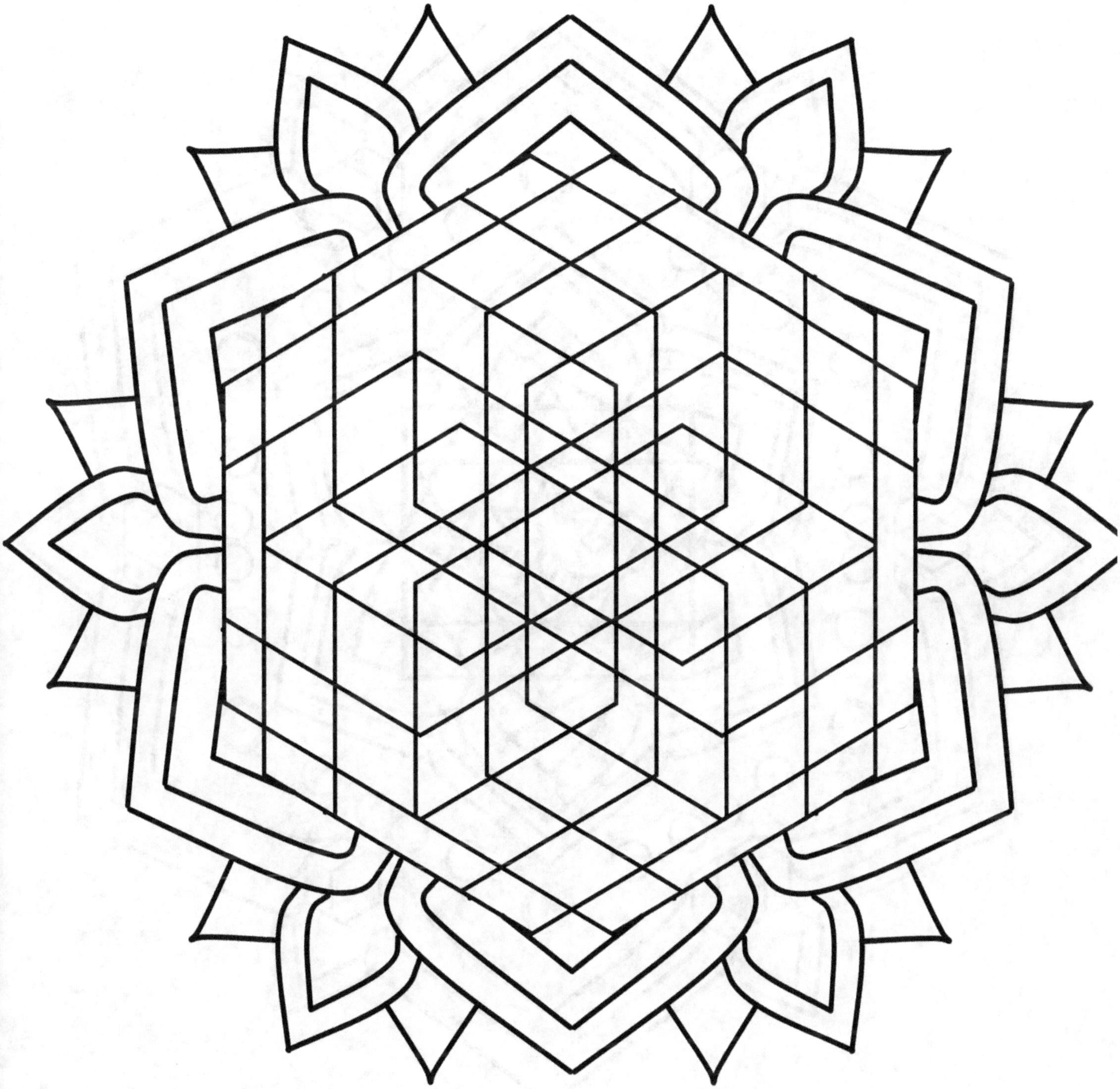

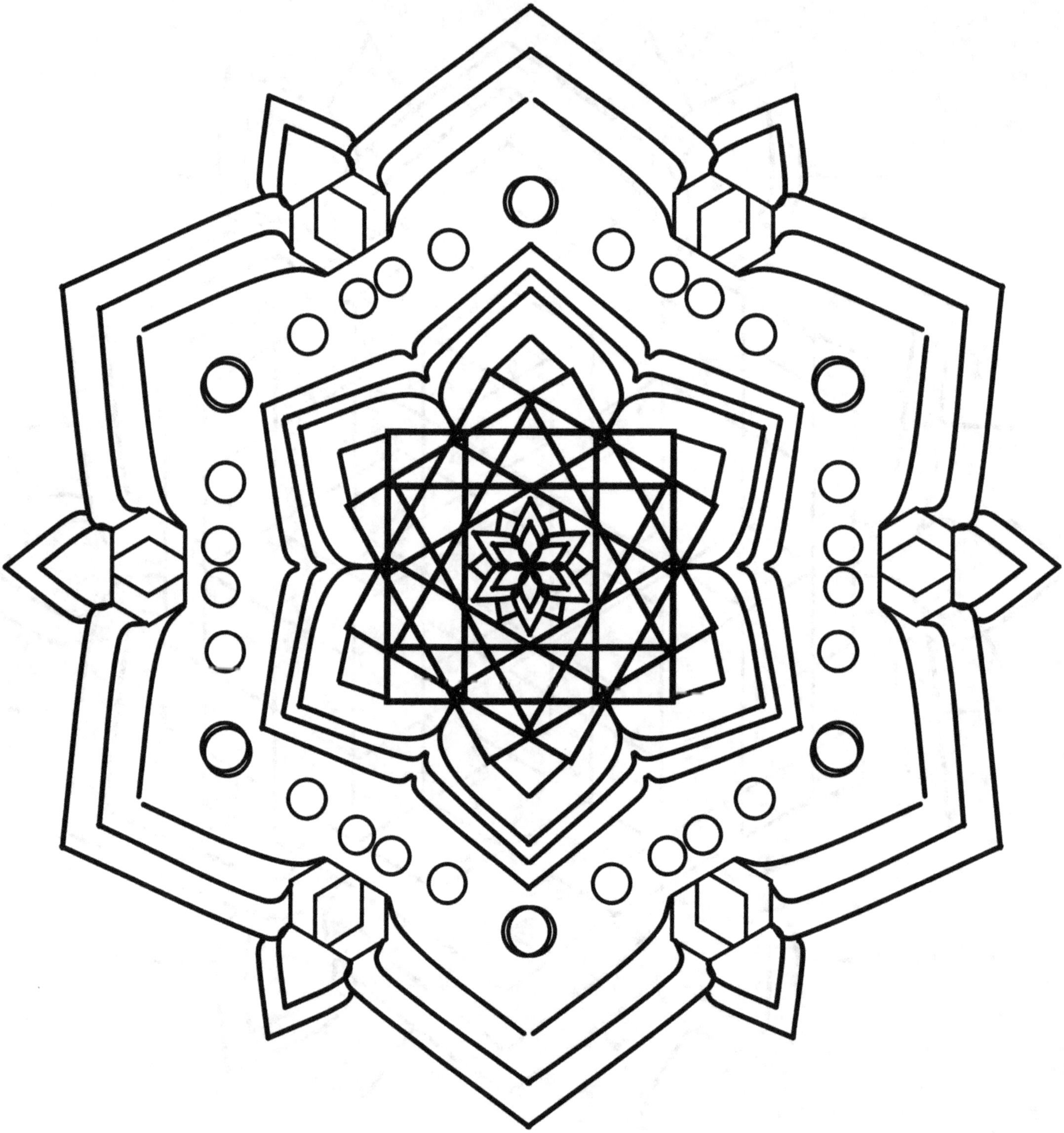

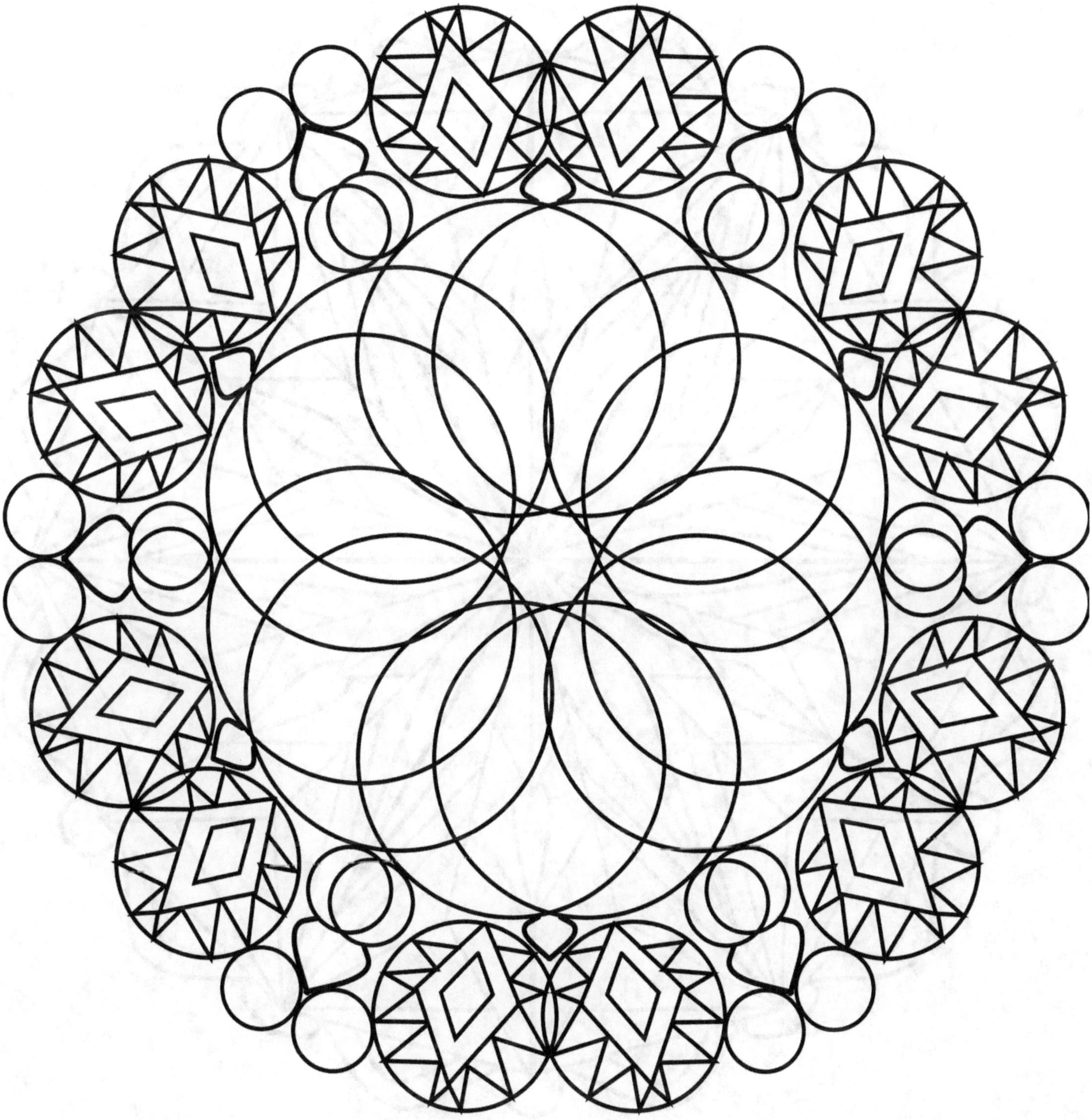

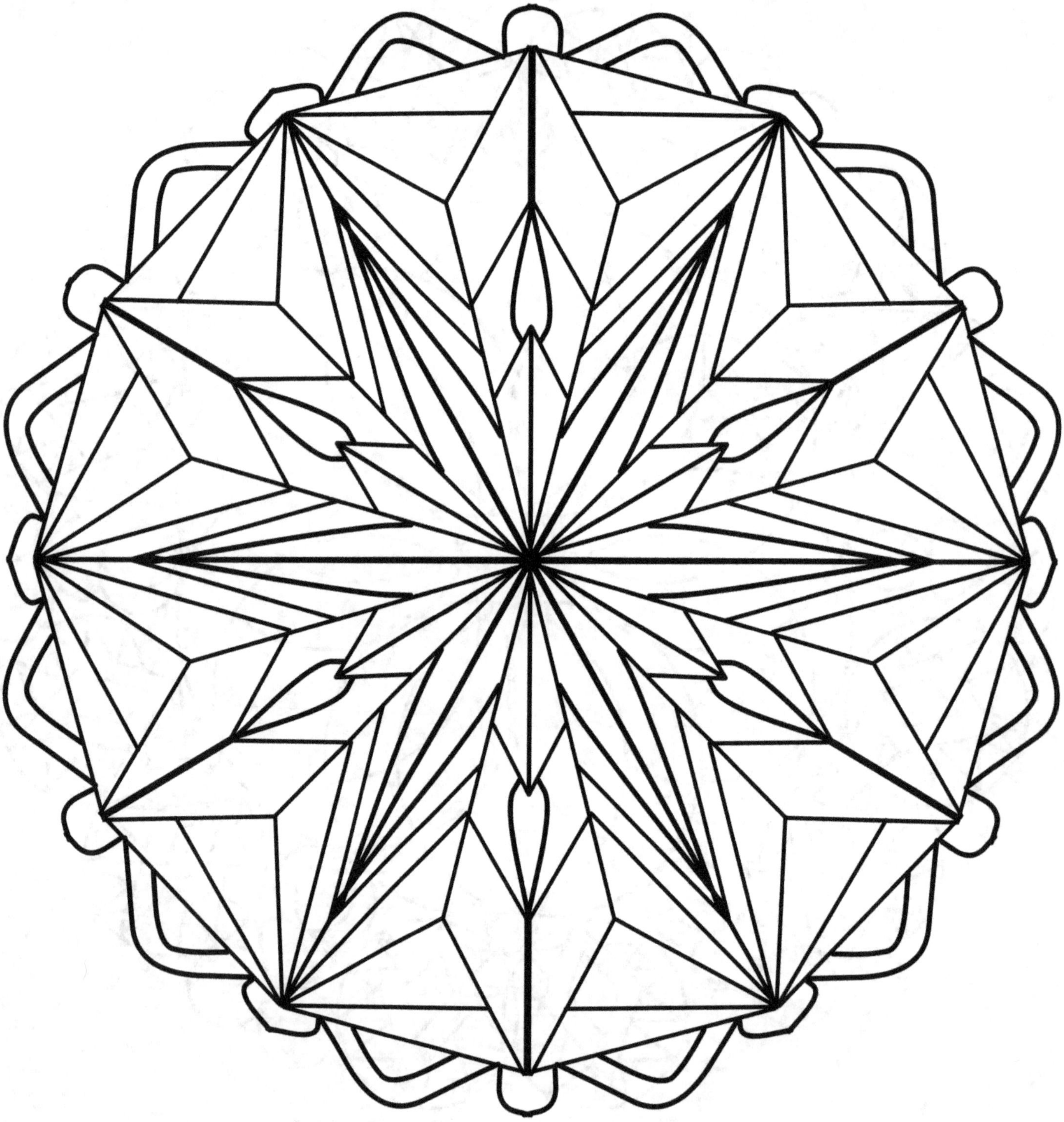

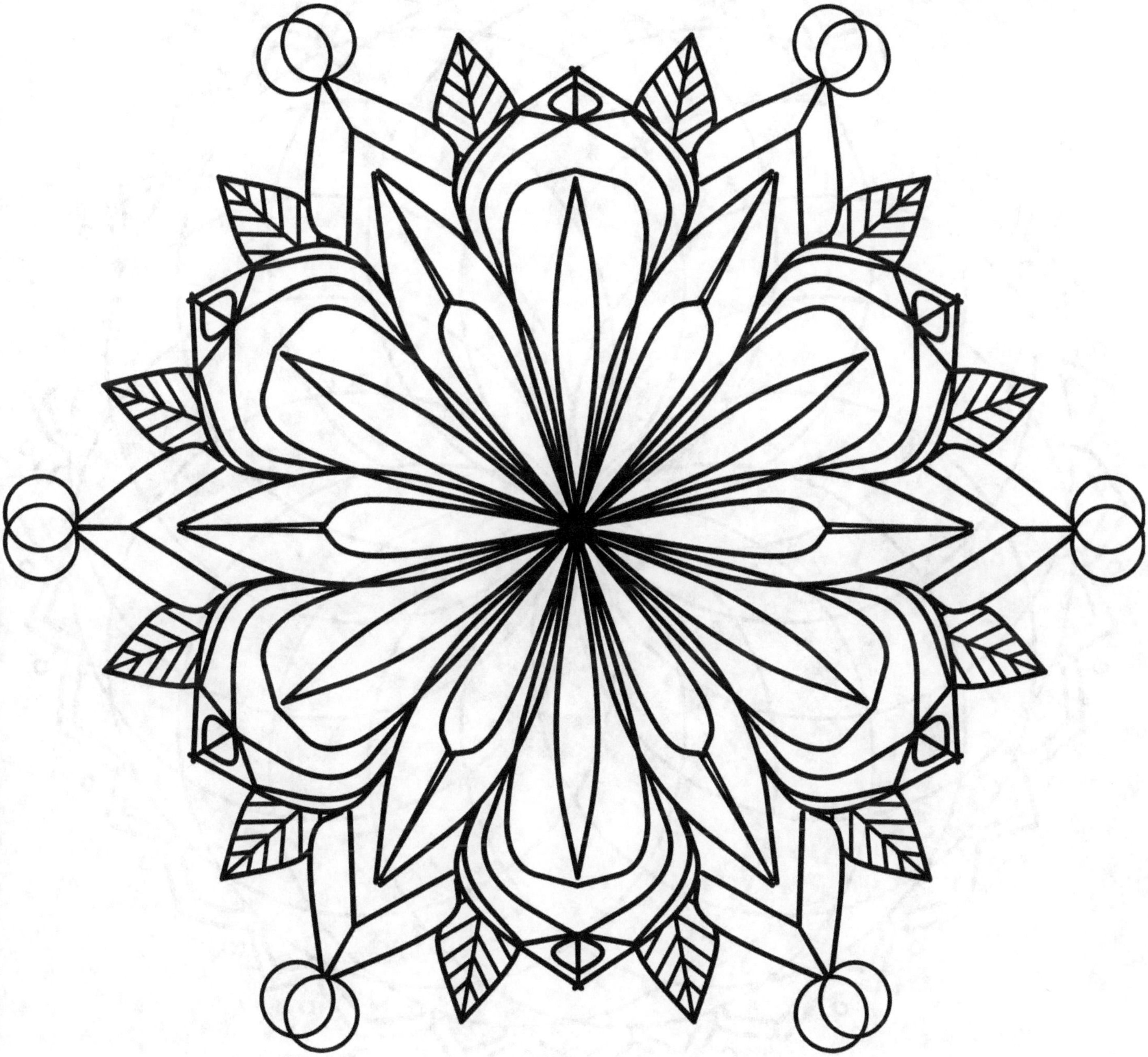

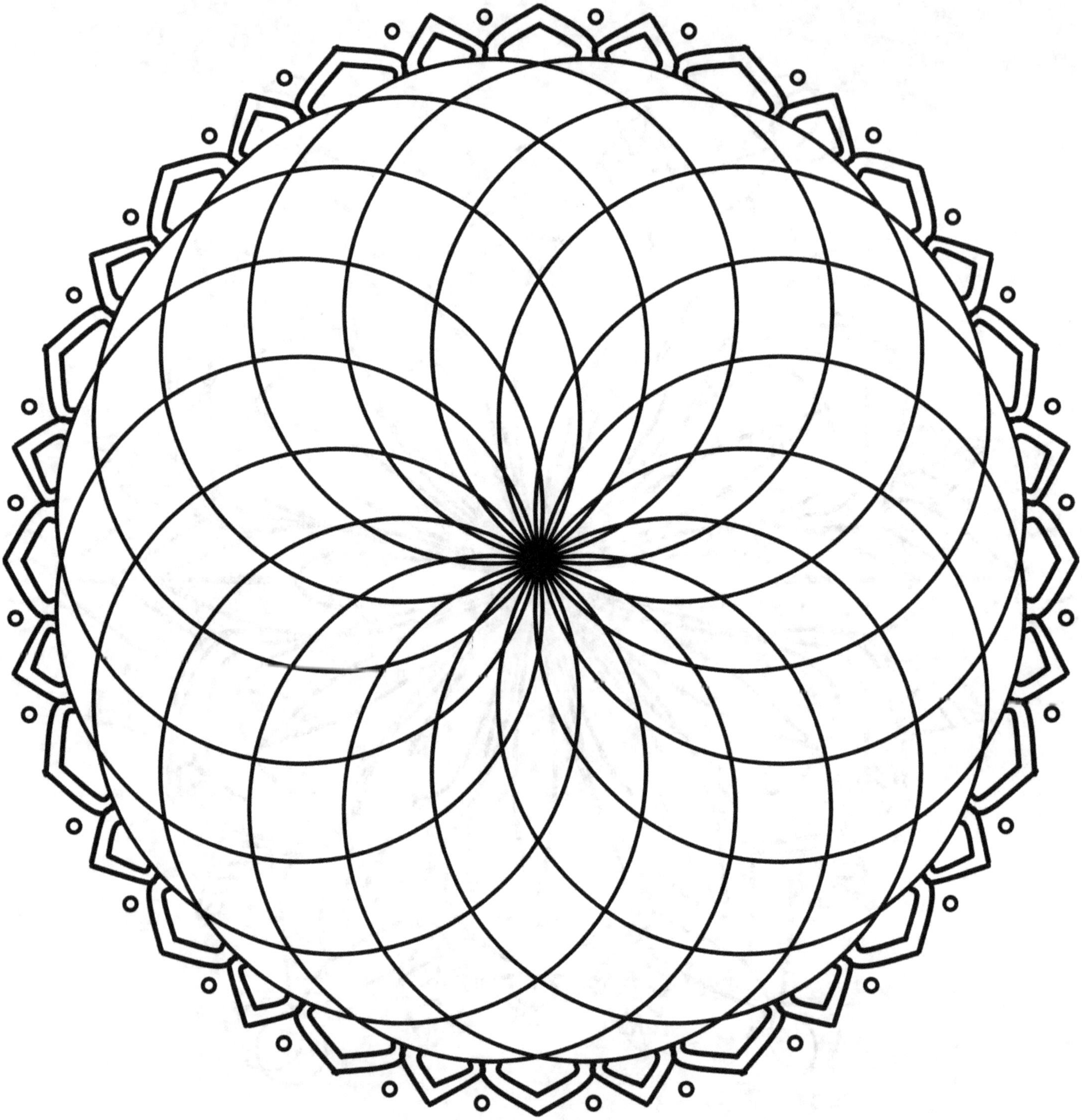

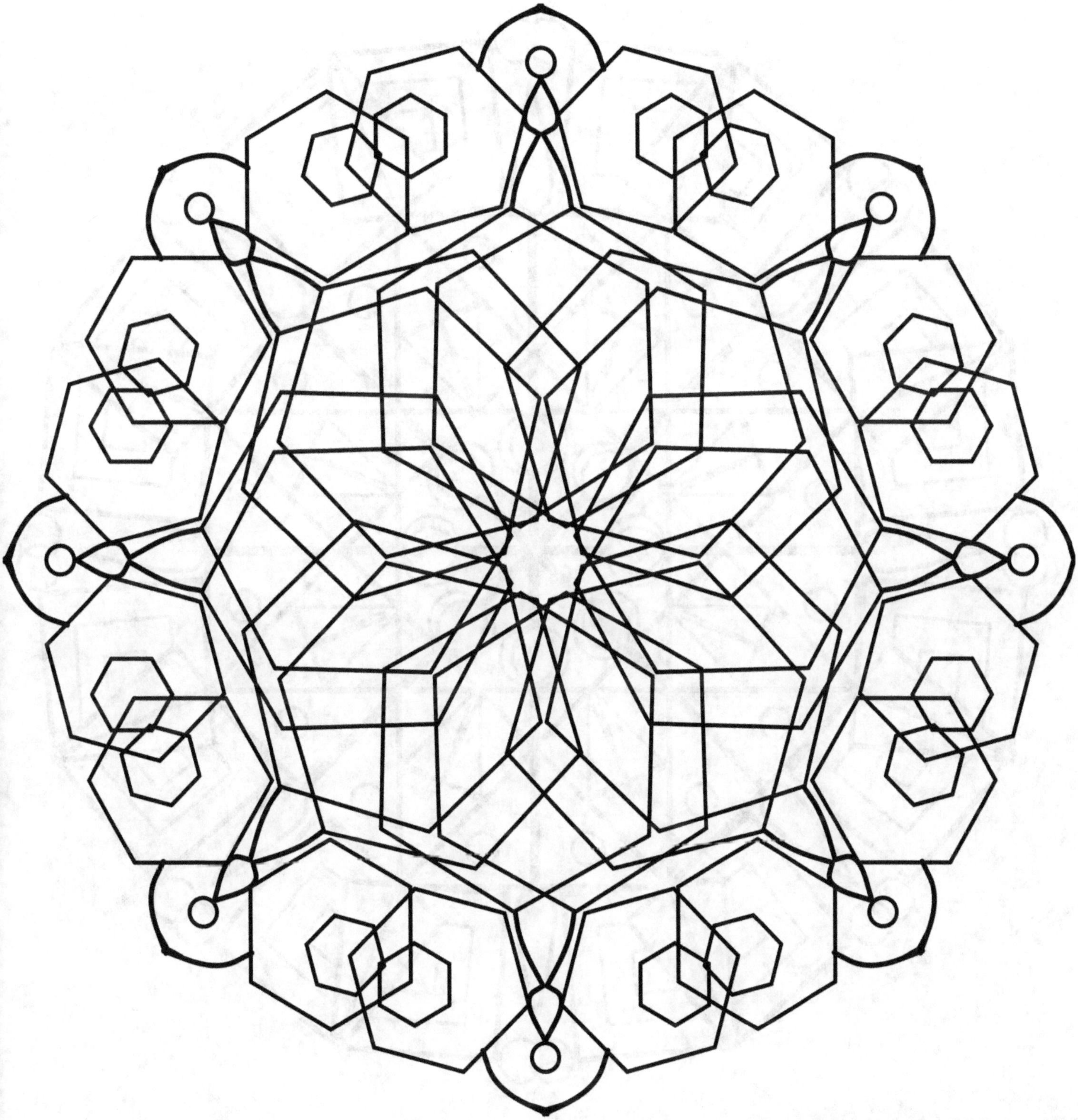

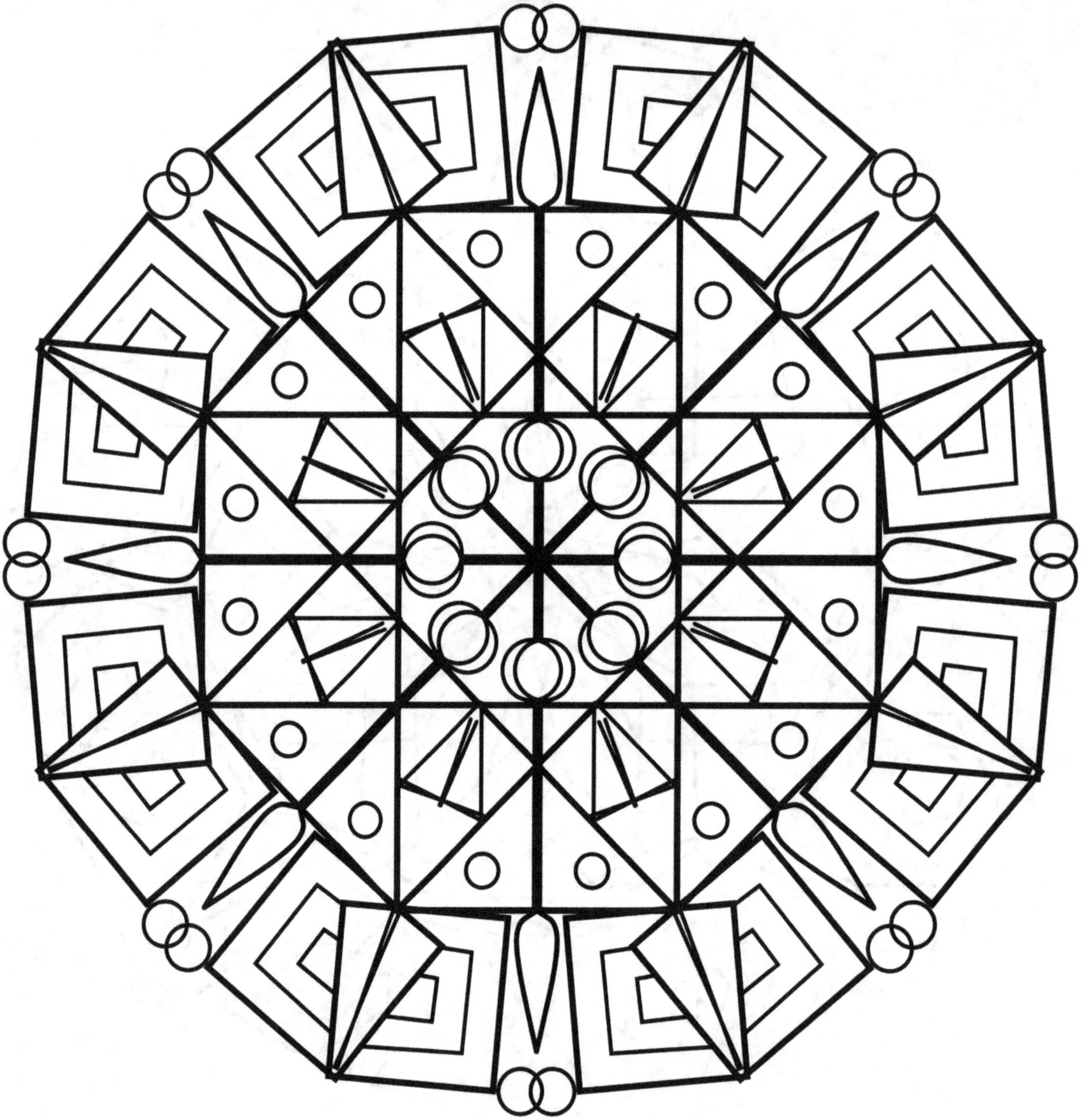

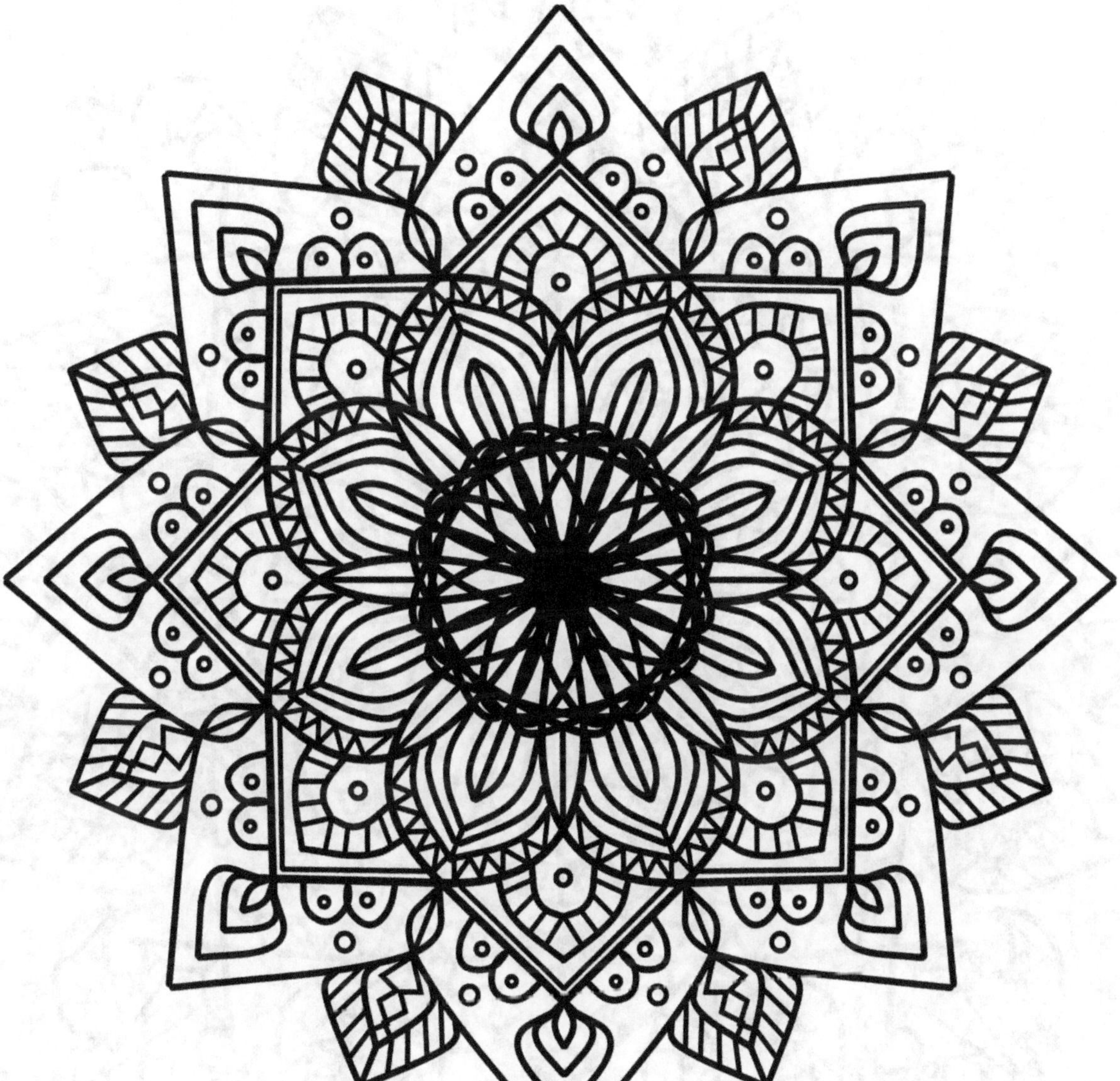

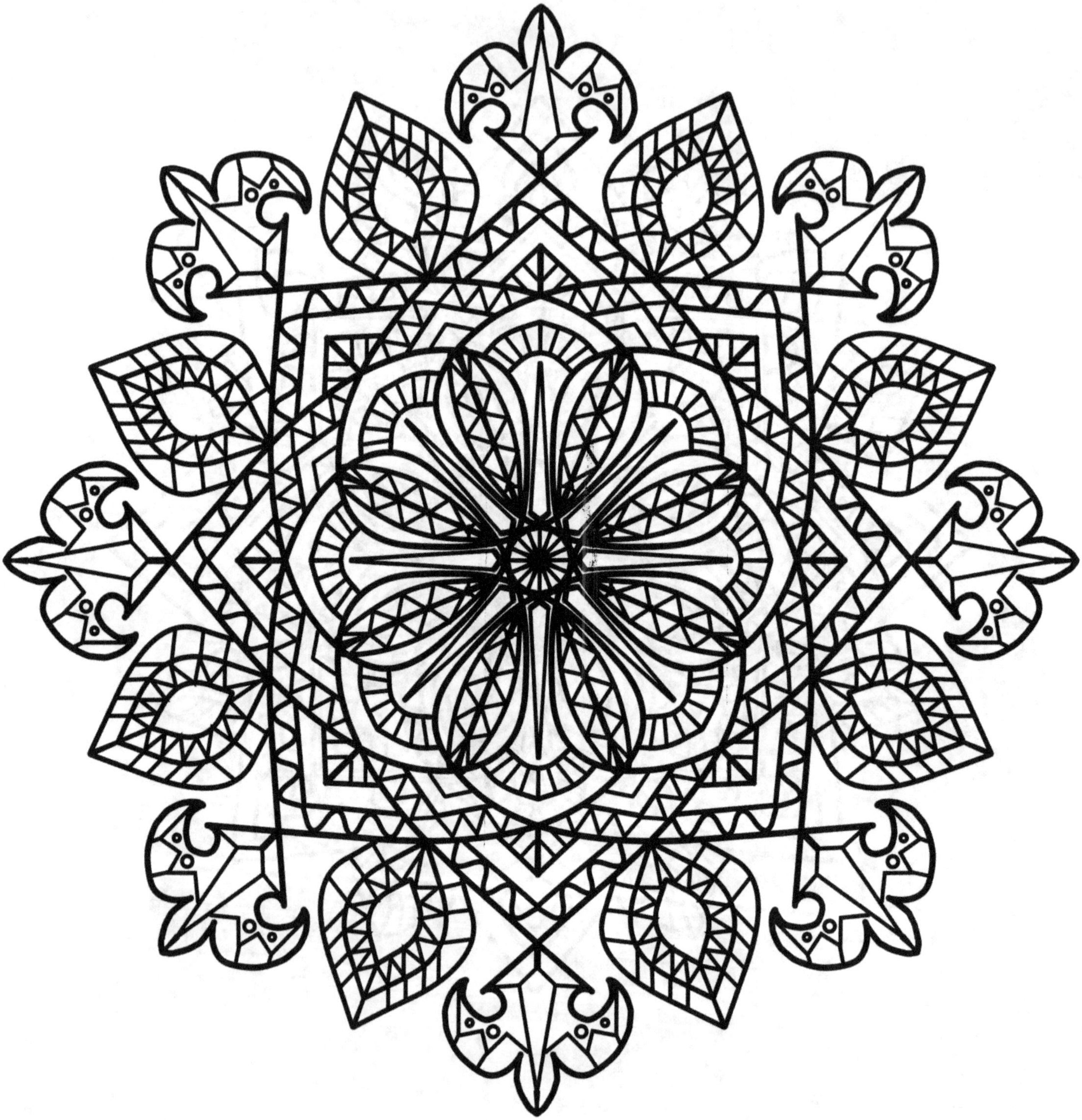

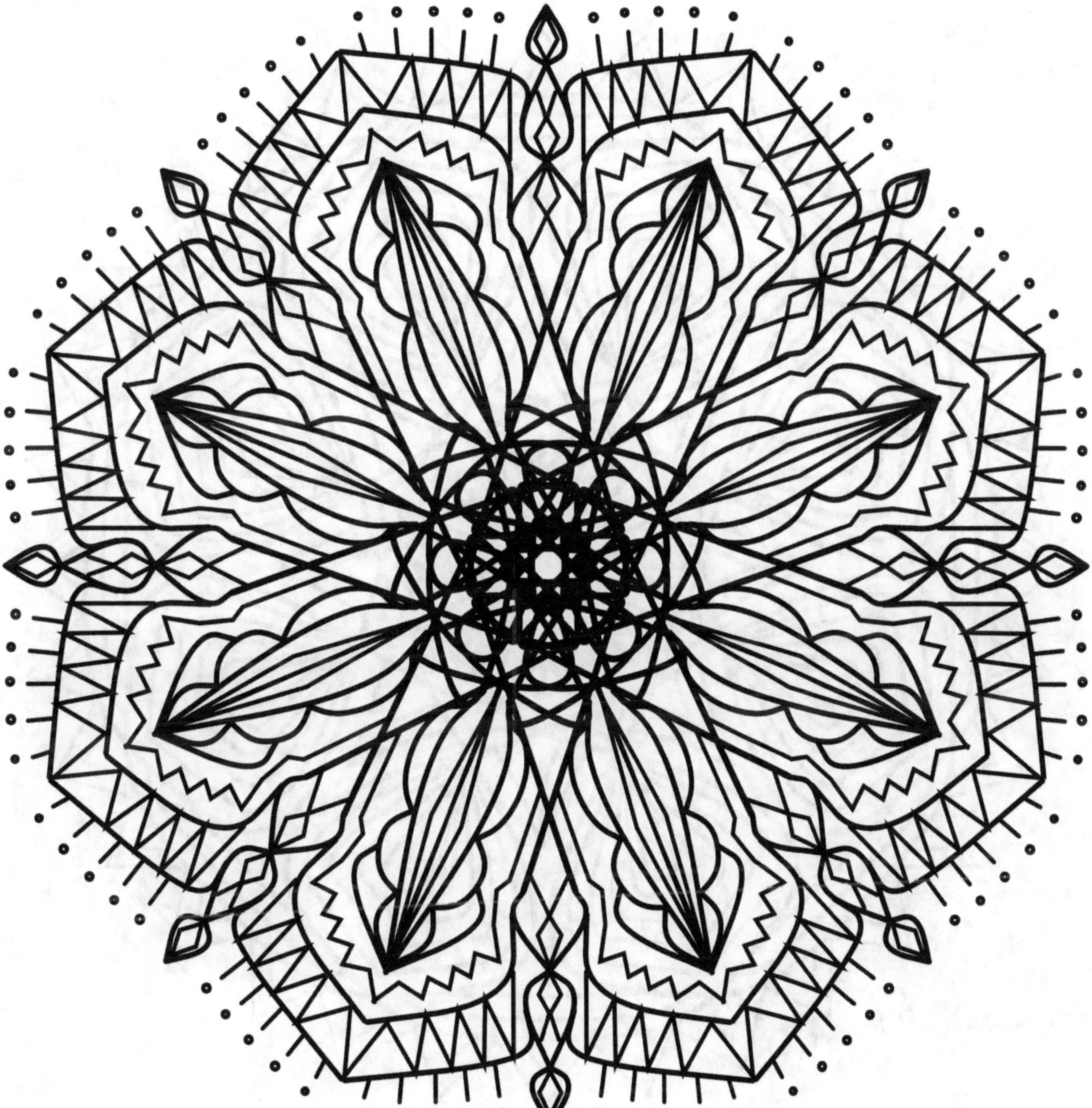

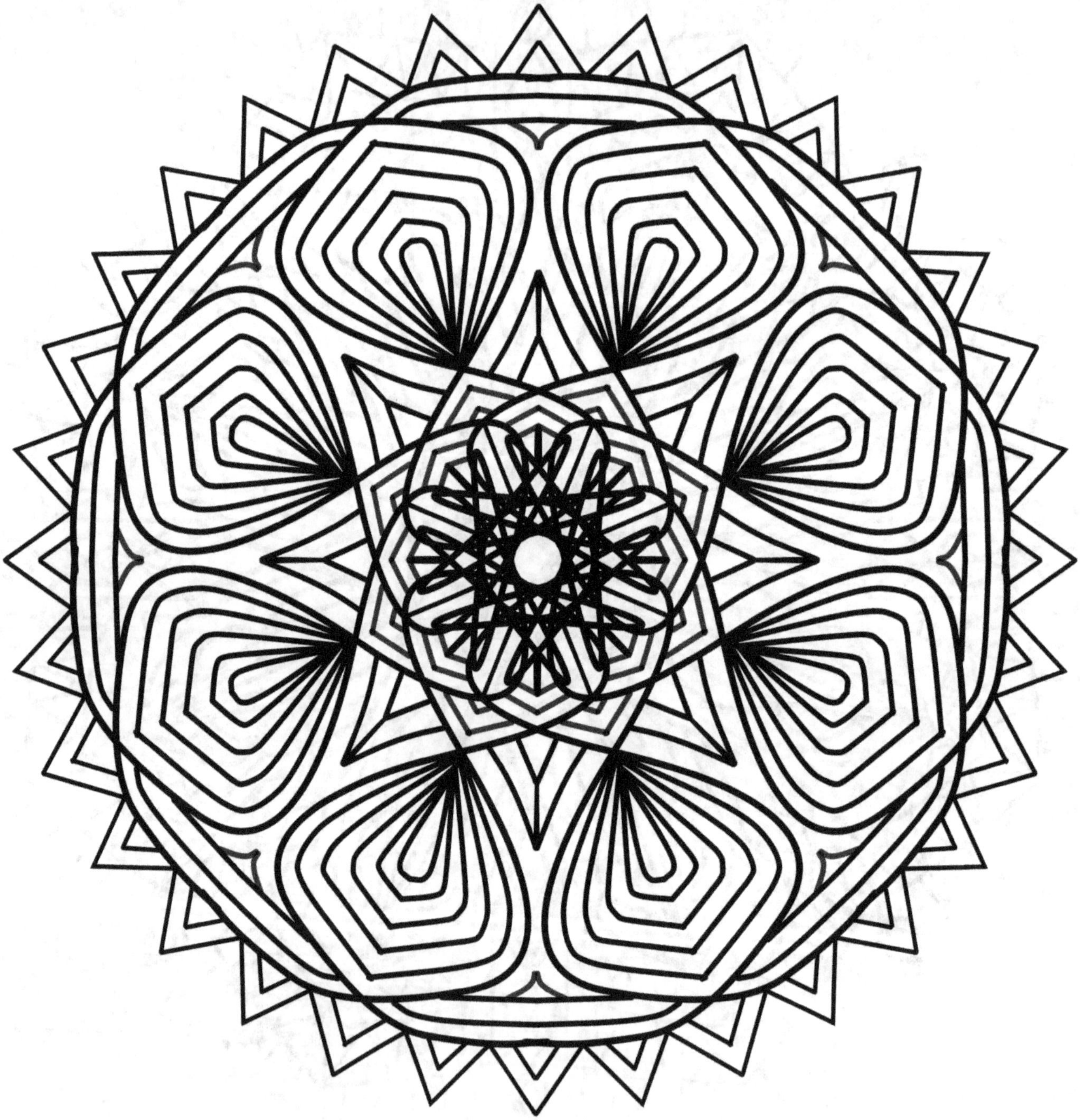

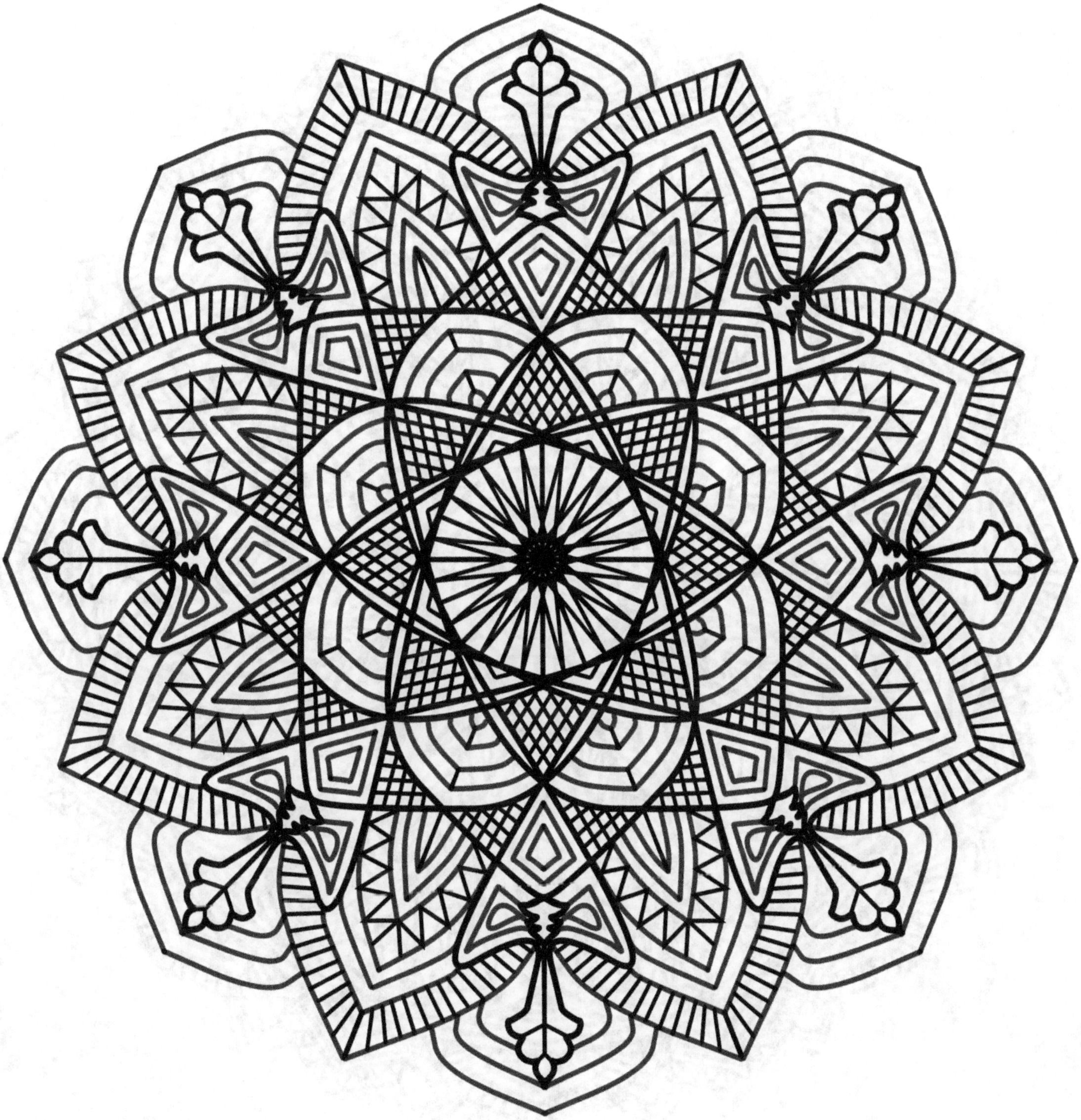

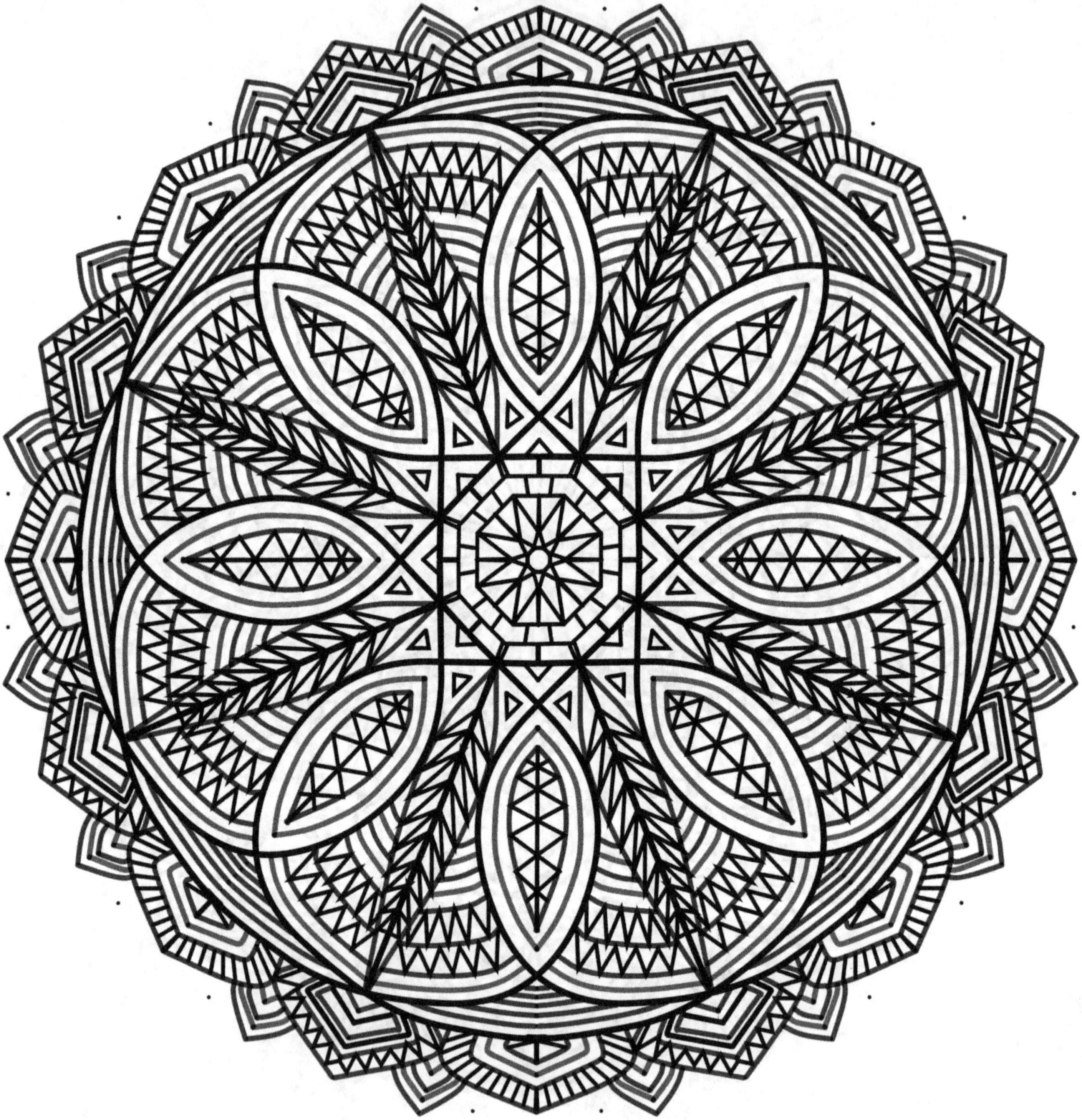

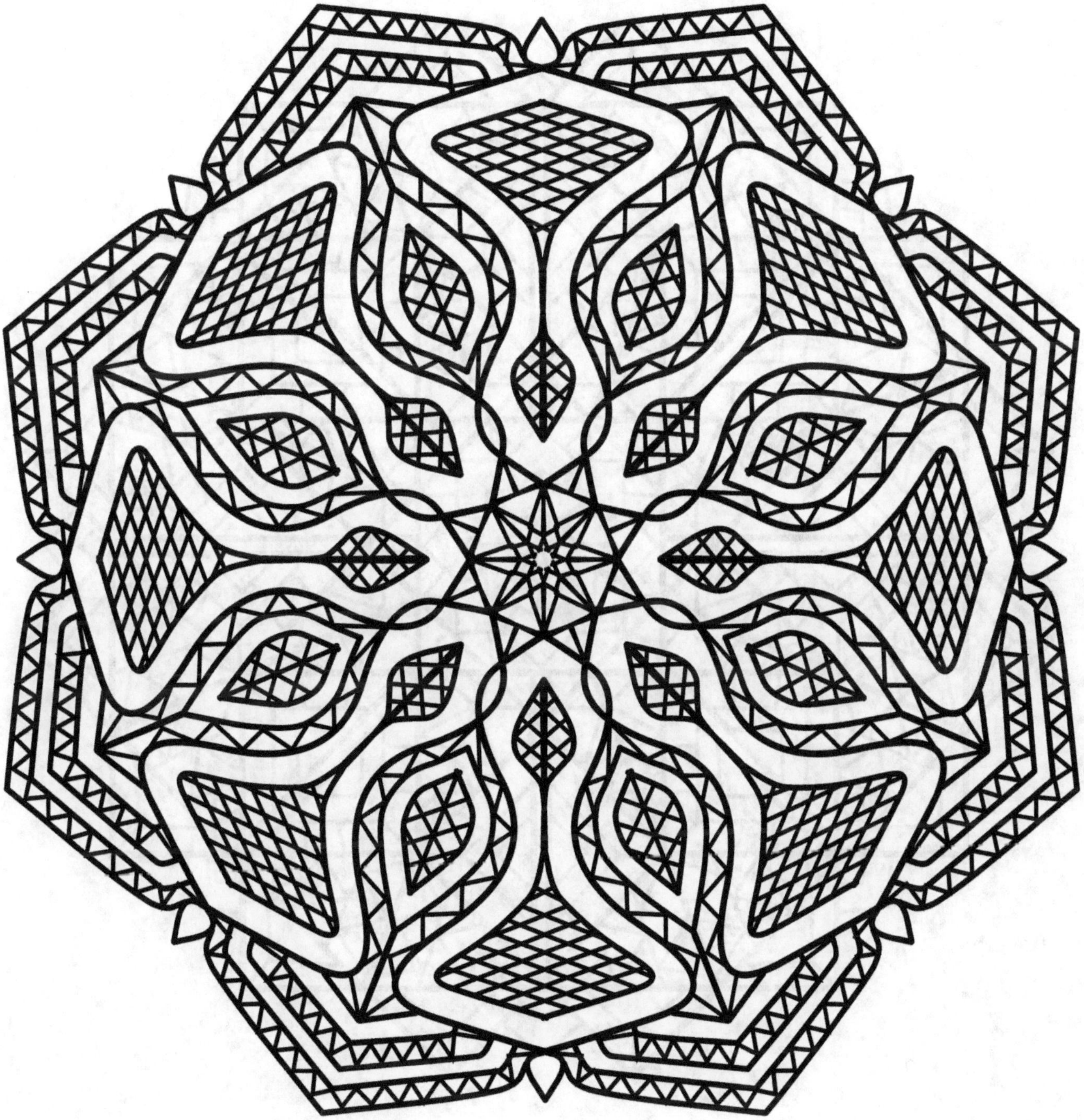

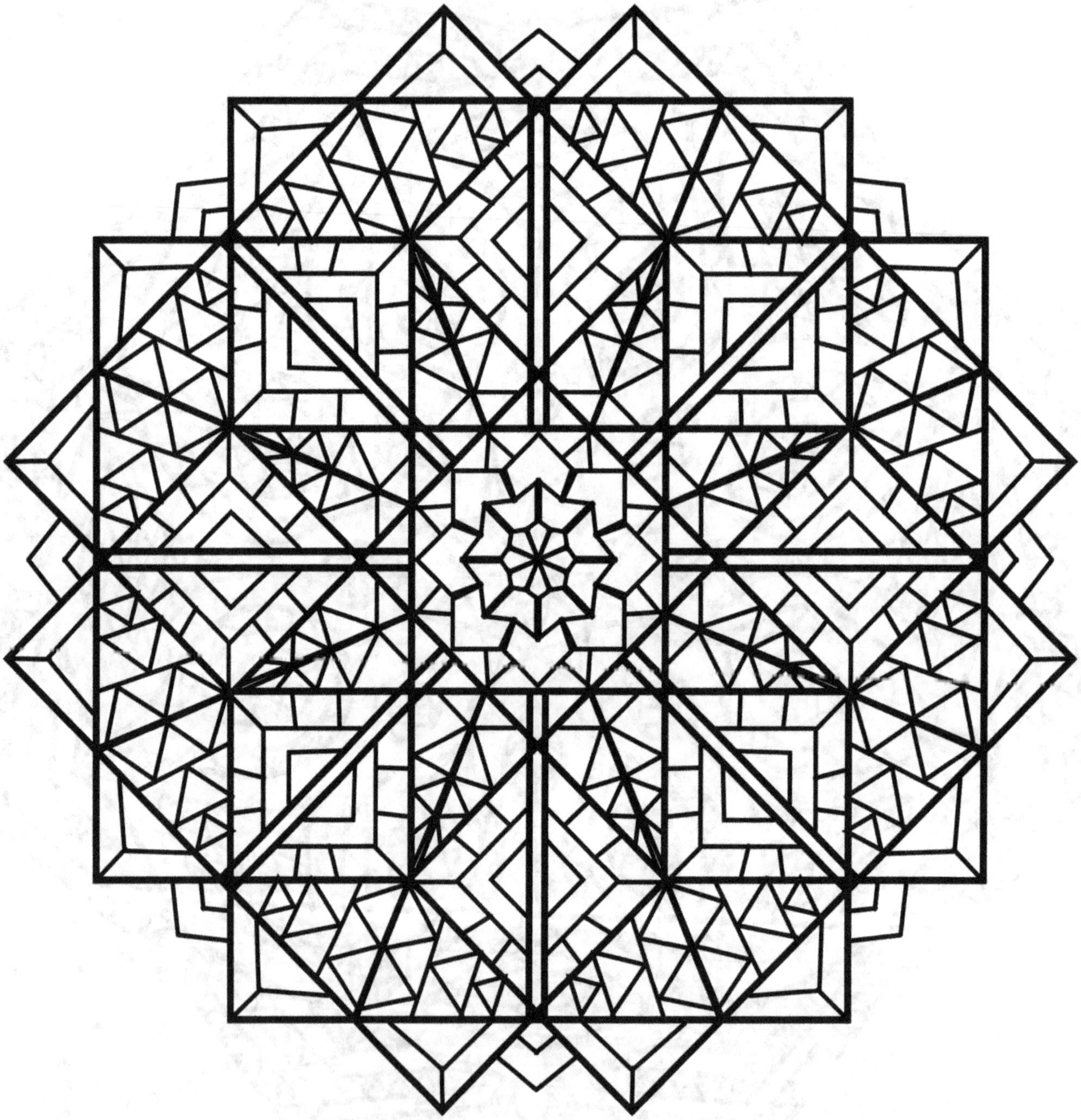

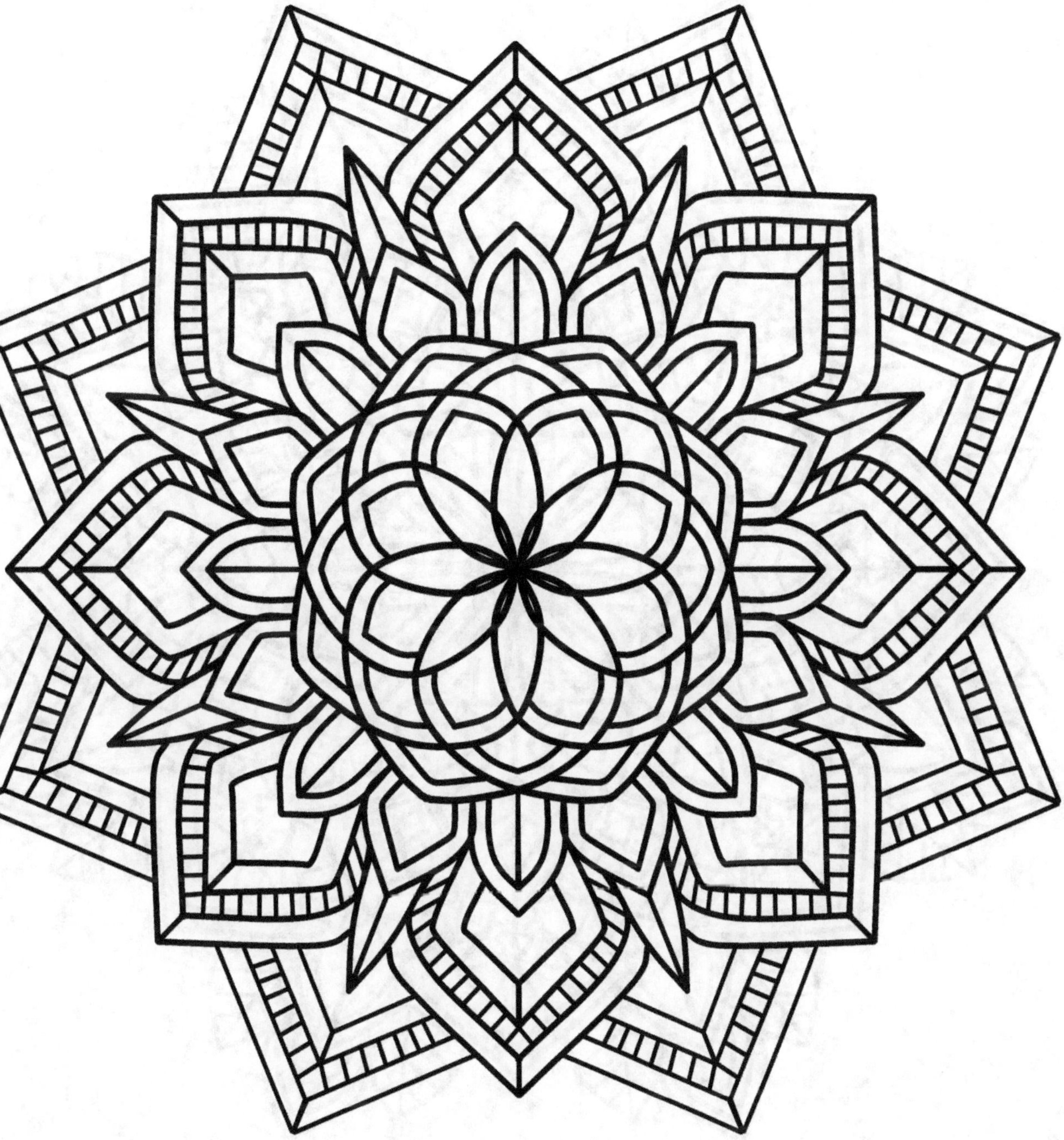

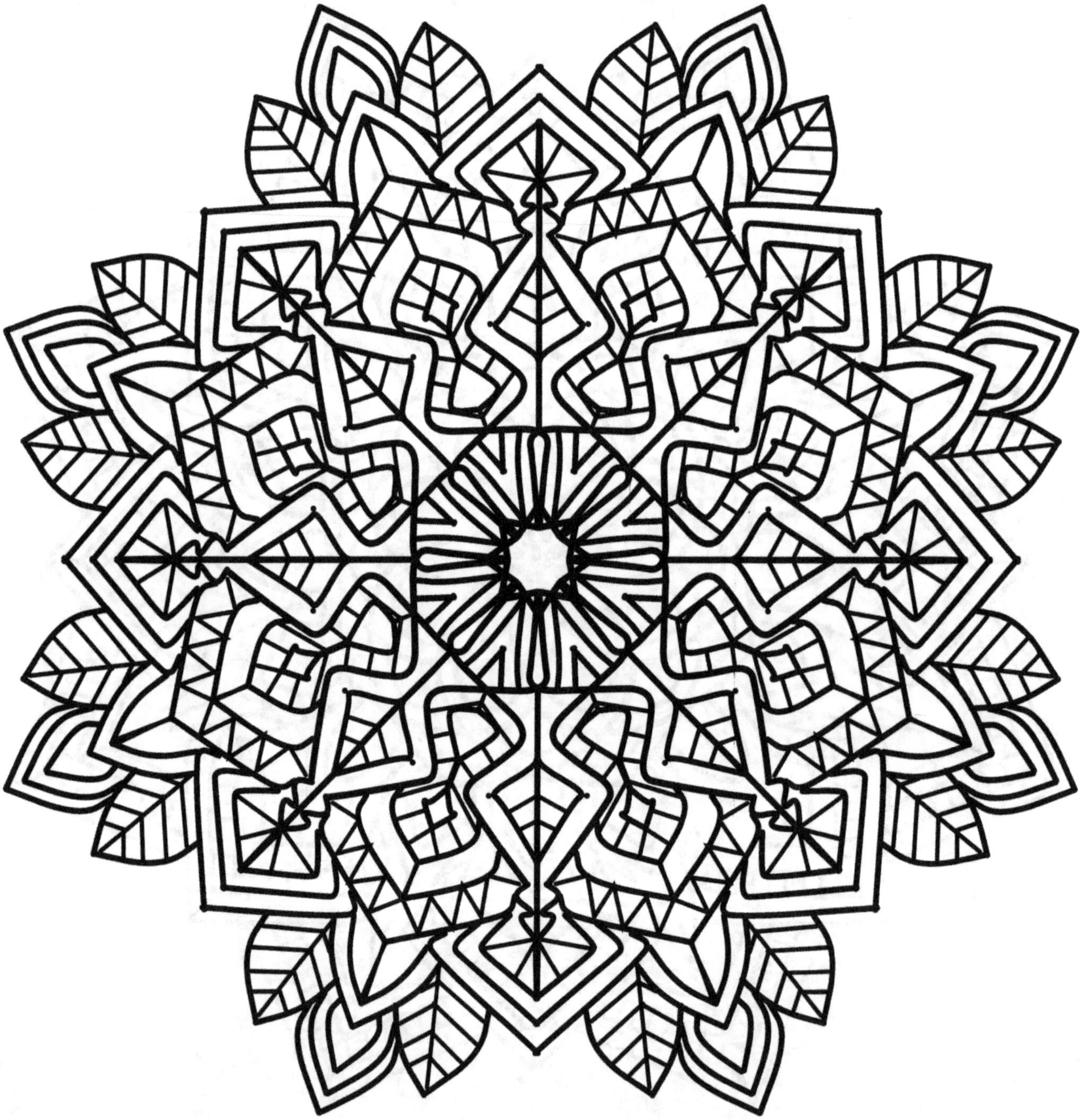

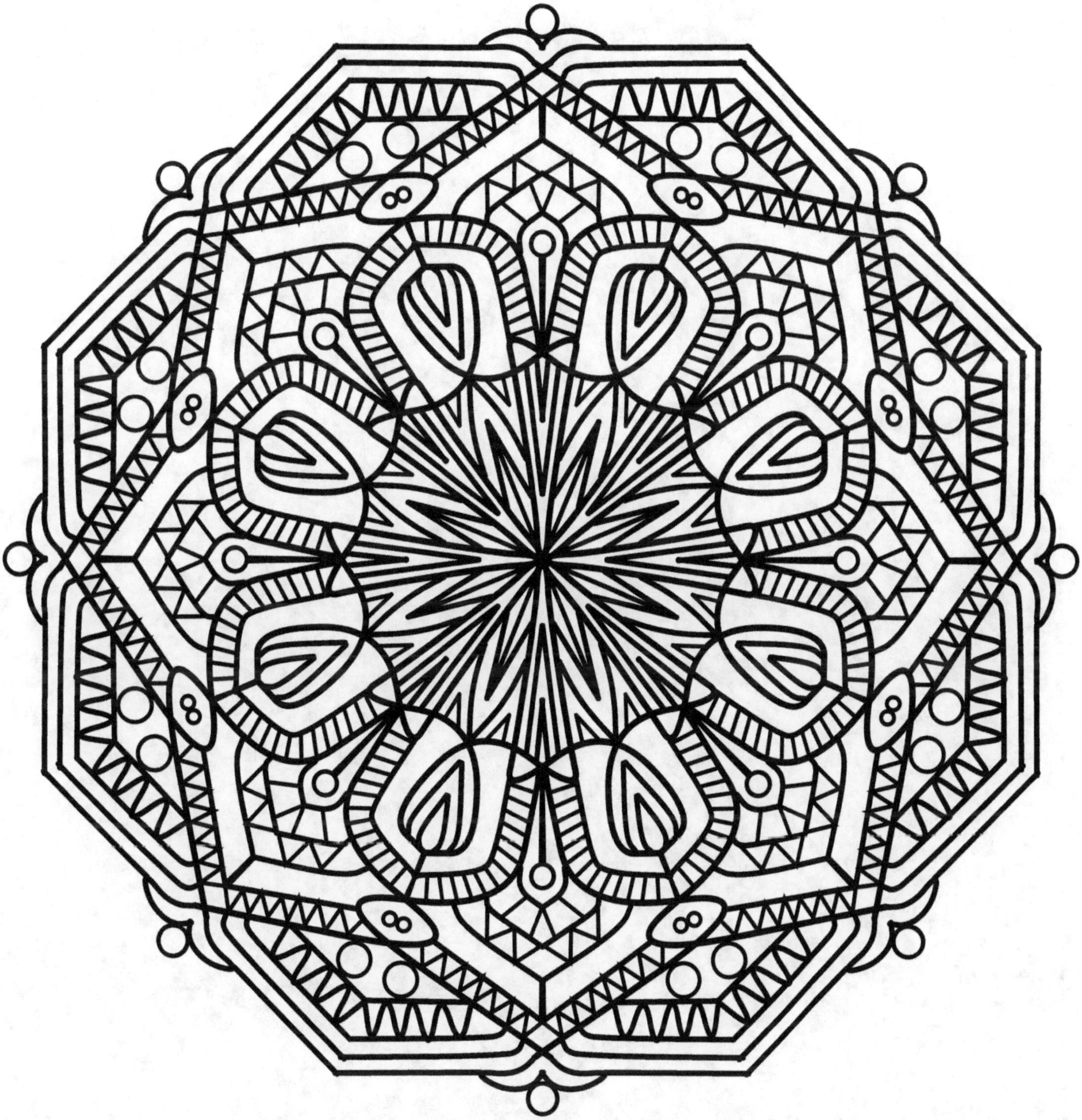

www.ingramcontent.com/pod-product-compliance
Lightning Source LLC
Chambersburg PA
CBHW081147170526
45158CB00009BA/2762
9781365622588